THE
SIX-FIGURE
WOMAN
AND HOW TO BE ONE
LOIS WYSE

LINDEN PRESS/SIMON & SCHUSTER   NEW YORK 1983

Copyright © 1983 by Garret Press
All rights reserved
including the right of reproduction
in whole or in part in any form
Published by Linden Press/Simon & Schuster
A Division of Simon & Schuster, Inc.
Simon & Schuster Building
Rockefeller Center
1230 Avenue of the Americas
New York, New York 10020
LINDEN PRESS/SIMON & SCHUSTER
and colophon are trademarks of
Simon & Schuster, Inc.
Designed by Karolina Harris
Manufactured in the United States of America
1   2   3   4   5   6   7   8   9   10
Library of Congress Cataloging in Publication Data
Wyse, Lois.
The six-figure woman, and how to be one.

1. Women executives.   I. Title.   II. Title: Six-
figure woman.
HF5500.2.W94   1983   658.4′09′024042   83-14942
ISBN 0-671-47764-1

FOR
THE MOST IMPORTANT
SIX FIGURES
IN MY LIFE:
LEE,
KATHERINE,
HENRY,
ROBERT,
DENISE
AND ROSE.

INTRODUCTION

I did not begin as a six-figure woman.

I began as a $30-a-week woman.

Reporter. *Cleveland Press.*

Ten years later my salary was $300 a week. By then, however, I was a copywriter-creative director-occasional account person-sometime telephone operator at Wyse Advertising, a business I founded with Marc Wyse.

By the time I reached five figures ($30,000 a year), I had two children and still answered phones occasionally.

When I reached six figures, the children and I were all old enough to count, and the agency was old enough (and big enough) to be counted among the top 100 in the United States.

I took over the management of our New York office, eventually became president of that office, and twenty-five years after we started the company became president of the corporation as well.

So, you see, I am not exactly an overnight six-figure success. Nor are most six-figure women. Executive women, on the average, have been with their companies thirteen years, according to the 1982 Korn/Ferry Profile of Senior Women Executives.

Not many of us senior women executives have found it easy, this business of Getting There, Being There, Staying There.

We old girls don't always have an old-boy network, and the new females don't always have a new-woman mentality.

There is no shortcut to either, yet there is a need for both. And the need is increasing because the world around us is changing fast.

In September 1981, seven women graduates of the Harvard Business School "dressed and determined and trained for success as no generation of women before" posed for a picture for *Newsweek*.

For those women that day and for the scores of women business-school graduates of the past decade, the question was, "How long will it take for me to get to the boardroom?" But early in 1982, the economy, male pressures, and women's own emotional needs combined to slow the fast track of the female achievers. A new pattern began to emerge, a direction that will create unexpected obstacles for career-oriented women in the 1980s. Instead of "How long will it take for me to become chairman?" women are beginning to accept reality and wonder, "Will I ever get to the boardroom?"

Women are still concentrated in low-paying, dead-end jobs.

Although women now make up 43% of America's work force, the U.S. Department of Labor reported in 1982 that "the discrepancy between the average earnings of men and women hasn't lessened over the past two decades." In fact, compared with men's wages, the Labor Department says that women earned proportionally less in 1983 than they did in 1955.

There is no real pressure to hire the executive woman.

The Republicans came to power in 1980 with no mandate from women voters.

ERA has failed to pass.

Fewer annual reports emphasize the concerns of women employees.

Newspapers no longer write front-page stories about NOW, and names like Bella Abzug and Gloria Steinem have all but disappeared from the media. Since you can judge public interest by front pages and TV news, it is safe to assume that the press believes the Women's Movement has turned into another garden club.

As a result of the economic climate, corporations are eliminating their so-called business frills.

During the corporate profit heydays of the 1970s, corporations responded to increasing public-opinion polls and opened their purses a little wider to spend what would otherwise have been tax dollars on women's consulting groups, scholarships for women, research and development on products directed to the new, intelligent, vocal working woman.

But as corporate profits wither so do women-oriented *pro bono* corporate benefits. Often they are the first to go.

The female corporate director is no longer important to the Fortune 500 companies. *The Corporate Director*, the journal of corporate governance, in its November/December 1982 issue, listed 70 new corporate directors, only three of whom were women.

There is an increasing number of women with high expectations and qualifications.

More women have been trained more extensively than ever before. The Harvard Business School reports an all-time high in female enrollment. In 1968 there were 30 women, 3.9 percent of the total enrollment. In 1973 there were 87 women, or 10.7 percent of the class. In 1982 the numbers jumped to 191 women, or 24.1 percent of the total.

And the Business School is but one example. At Harvard Law School women make up 34 percent of the enrollment (up from 5 percent in the 1960s). At Stanford

Law School 27 percent of the 1982 graduating class was female.

Male and female college students now share the same goals for careers and family life, according to a five-year cooperative research project measuring goals, values, and interests of students from Barnard, Bryn Mawr, Mount Holyoke, Radcliffe-Harvard, Smith, Vassar, and Wellesley.

The study of the seven colleges shows that in the early 1970s most female students at the seven schools aspired to careers in the traditional women's fields—social work and teaching. By the 1980s only 3 percent of the 8,000 female students surveyed had similar aspirations. One-third of these students were planning to pursue careers in medicine, law, business, and, according to *The New York Times*, "other fields that were once restricted to men."

So even though the number of trained women is increasing, the number of jobs for which they are trained is not.

Women are learning that an elitist education does not guarantee a position at the top.

Women lawyers argue that their failure to make a dent in the profession's power structure is both an indictment of the justice system and a failure to maximize a valuable resource.

The National Law Journal surveyed 151 of the country's largest law firms and reported in June 1982 that 32 had no women partners, 106 had no black partners, and 133 had no Latino partners. Women make up 17 percent of the lawyers in these firms, yet only 3 percent are partners.

Eleanor Holmes Norton, the Georgetown University Law School professor and former chairman of the Equal Employment Opportunity Commission, said in

The Washington Post, "... women and minorities have had the bad luck to have gotten access to the profession at a time the bottom fell out of the market." She recommends that women study science, not law.

By 1990 there will be a glut of female managerial talent vying for the highest jobs in the new technology and information industries.

Women now form a disproportionate ratio in white-collar and information industries, the so-called new technology. Coupled with the decline of production and old technology companies, more and more women have been crowding the corridors in the new businesses. Consequently, within fifteen years we will see the largest number of qualified women in history reaching for a handful of top jobs.

As a result, by the late 1980s the business climate will be the toughest ever for the most qualified, achievement-oriented, experienced women the world has ever produced.

Promotions will be given, but women will have to fight hard. It will take unusual talent, drive, and human skills to make it even to an entry-level job in many fields, and chances are that the word "assistant" will appear in a first-job description.

But *assistant* is not where the determined woman wants to be.

Like the men of preceding generations, she regards her career as an extension of herself. She wants to be more than good; she wants to be better. She wants to do more than work for a salary; she wants to work to enhance her own sense of worth to society and to herself.

In short, she is searching always for those things that will get her there faster, keep her there longer, and satisfy her unlimited dreams in a limiting world.

I

$25,000 OR LESS: THE STARTING GATE

Optimistic, energetic, scared.

If you are entering the business world, those words probably describe you.

You are excited about the publicized opportunities for women and willing to work long hours, but you are afraid that you may be ten years too early—or ten years too late—to make it to the top.

You are, in all likelihood, a recent college graduate, have yet to earn your MBA. You think you may want to go back to school at night, not necessarily to earn another degree but to take those courses appropriate to advancing your career.

You probably were active in campus affairs, are not married, but you have had at least one serious relationship and you assume you will eventually marry. You also assume you will have children, but are not certain exactly how you will manage your career when you do. You are determined that some time after starting your family you will go back to work.

Your parents are generally supportive of your career aspirations, just as they were of your educational aspirations. You are not sure what you want to be "when you grow up." You are certain of only one thing: you don't want to be like your mother.

As you interview for a variety of jobs, you will become less sanguine about your opportunities. You will feel less optimistic and more scared. How can you possibly have experience when no one will give it to you?

By the fourteenth interview, you will be somewhat perplexed.

What do employers want?

What are the qualities that will make someone hire you instead of one of the other graduates (all of whom seem far more formidable competition now than they did when you were in school)?

The major qualities employers seek are very much the same, regardless of the type of business. In talking with other executives, these are the qualities mentioned again and again:

1. Character

There is no substitute for it. You have been identifying it, developing it and shaping it all your life. And by now you have it or you don't. It is that combination of morals, ethics, and personal standards that makes you the person you are.

2. Goals

I like to ask people what they want to do eventually, what business they really want to be in and what role they hope to assume. When they're without goals, I'm reluctant to hire. If they want my job, all the better.

3. Energy

A high energy-level is important. People who handle their jobs with apparent ease will always be considered for extra or larger assignments.

4. Commitment

Commitment is that passion in business that comes from a sense of caring, the willingness to function in or out of the spotlight, depending on the job. You see it in someone who shoulders responsibility and is willing to see a job through (very old-fashioned words).

Caring and commitment go together like ambition and talent.

5. **Unique talents**
Because there is no substitute for talent, employers look always for those talents which are helpful in their business or which they may not have previously considered for their business—talents that will give a company a different perspective on what it does.

6. **Personality**
No matter what the job, it is better performed when talent and skills are accompanied by a pleasant personality (that means someone who can smile, who radiates warmth without oozing charm). Of course you know what personality is all about. Just make sure that when you seek a job, you don't show too much or too little.

7. **Luck and brains**
It takes luck to put you in a certain place at a certain time—and it takes brains for you to know what to do once you're there.

8. **Attitude**
Intense determination and refusal to accept the words "It can't be done" are as necessary to success as education and experience. Success is possible only when you know it is not impossible.

Mind your p's and q's.
Not everyone is meant to be a six-figure woman. So before you reach, ask yourself a few questions.
• Do you have the spirit to make it to the top?
• Do you have the background to push on as the next six-figure woman?

Ambition and desire are not enough. Before you make the run, know your p's and q's. The p's are your positive attributes. The q's are your questionables.

Here's a simple little quiz you can score yourself.

FACT	P (ositives)	Q (uestionable)	Negative
Education	Score 6 for any advanced degree plus 1 for each year of experience since school.	Score 5 for bachelor's degree.	-5 for high school only; score 1 for each year of college.
Choice of Job	Score 8 for new technology; score 6 for information; score 5 for service.	Score 3–5 for production companies.	-5 for the arts (dance, theater, music, painting).
Experience	Score 6–10 for managerial position in chosen field.	Score 1–5 for each year of experience in chosen or related business.	-3 for no experience.
Age	21–22; score 10. 23–24; score 9. 25–26; score 8. 27–28; score 7. 29–30; score 6.	30–33; score 5. 34–37; score 4. 38–41; score 3. 42–45; score 2. 46–48; score 1.	-1 for each over 50.
Contacts	Family-owned business; score 6–10 depending on size of company.	Special "in"; score 1–5 depending on relationship.	Take a -1 for lack of personal contacts.

To compute your score, add the p's and q's; subtract the negatives. Anything over 35 is a shoo-in for success. If you score 25 to 35, chances are you can make it. At 15 to 25 you still have a shot at the top. Under 15, you'd better reconsider—change fields, go back to school, get more experience.

Some of the things every successful woman knows about business are in this book, for it is based on the advice of women—and some men—who have made it to the magic six figures.

≡ **If you're trying to decide between two jobs, go to work for the company that already has at least one woman vice-president.**

Beware of any company that survived the '60s and '70s without ever increasing responsibilities and salaries of women. Chances are if they didn't do it during those years when the pressures were greatest, they'll be even more reluctant during the '80s.

If you want to know how difficult it is to get to the top, remember that only one woman heads a Fortune 500 company. She is Katharine Graham of the *Washington Post*, who inherited her job and then had the chance to prove her business acumen.

≡ **Assess the job realistically.**

One of the dangers of a new job is that we women often see it in extremes: we think everything about it is a disaster or we think it's all one big love fest.

We may look at a job and see only negatives (we hate them/they hate us) because so many of us insulate ourselves for rejection. Then when it comes we shrug and say, "I knew it would happen." But it doesn't have to happen.

That doesn't mean thinking all is perfect. Just look at the job realistically.

◉ Don't be a snob about your job.

So you don't work in the chairman's office, and the president doesn't seek your advice daily—is that any reason to disparage the job?

No, says Melanie Kahane, whose interior design firm is one of the most famous in the world. "I was once a saleswoman at Bamberger's in New Jersey; I sketched for a fashion house; I did brochures for a girls' school. They seemed like unimportant jobs, but each one taught me so much.

"What women must recognize," says Kahane, "is that they do have a drive, a need to succeed, and most of us know how it originated. My drive was the result of my parents' difficult financial situation. We had lived in Sioux Falls, and then one day five out of the seven banks in town closed. We were forced to move East where Mother had well-to-do relatives. My uncle sent me to school, but humbled me because I always had to go to him to ask for my allowance. Each time I did it I swore I would never again go hat in hand to anyone. And I haven't."

◉ No matter what the job description says, your real job is to make the boss look good.

It doesn't matter if it's not part of your job description— do it anyway. If you're asked to go to the bank or sharpen a pencil—do it, and do it with grace.

≡ Be honest with your boss.

Unless women deal honestly with their male bosses, there will be a great tendency to discount women in business.

Arrelle von Hurter, an account executive with E. F. Hutton who now works in London, says, "When I started in business ten years ago, I let my boss know that I wanted to have my first child by the time I was thirty. That meant that, although I would continue to work and do my best in a normal workday, I didn't want a job that would require travel or unusually long hours. I was honest; as much as I dreamed of working in mergers and acquisitions, I knew I wouldn't have the time to travel or work the late hours that part of the work requires.

"Instead I became a broker, but I know that my management trusts me now, and when my children are grown, the opportunity will be there for me."

≡ Remember: the salary is only one reward of business.

The opportunity to learn is an even greater reward.

Kathleen St. Johns, now creative director of Columbia Pictures TV, recalls that when she went to Columbia two years ago, she was willing to do anything to learn. "I'd clean files, sit in on meetings, anything that might teach me something.

"I'm always looking for good teachers," she said, "because no matter how much you learn in school, there are new lessons in every job."

● Sharpen your secretarial skills.

Now that we hold women executives in high regard, we seem to hold secretarial skills in low regard.

I've never seen anyone, from sales managers to TV personalities, who wouldn't do her or his job quicker and better with improved typing, the ability to take shorthand, and a basic understanding of filing systems. Robert Broadbent, the president of Higbee's, the Cleveland-based department store, says that the greatest learning experience of his life was the time he spent as secretary to Cyrus Eaton, the world-famous industrialist. And the only reason Broadbent won the job over other applicants was that he knew how to type.

● Remember that talent alone won't advance your career.

If you told me I could choose between two people, one with limited talent and great discipline and the other with unlimited talent and no discipline, I'd hire the disciplined person. Because I've learned that talent grows. If you're young and caring and apply yourself and keep learning, something happens to your talent. It grows and expands. But if you have no discipline, your talent dries faster than rain on a hot sidewalk.

● Read the trade journals.

They'll give you a better background in your business than two more years of college.

● Be fair, never cheap.

It's smart to be thrifty; it's dumb to be cheap.

Whenever you cost a project, make sure that the person doing it for you has built his profit into the price, and make certain that the profit is a satisfactory one.

If you don't, you may find that the lowest bidder gives you the lowest quality.

◖ Don't confuse people with facts.

Don't throw statistics around like confetti.

One barefaced fact will convince more persuasively than seventeen fancy-worded overkill support statements.

◖ Don't let rejection stop your forward movement.

At some time everyone faces rejection from parents, teachers, or society. But, like Carol Goldberg, executive vice-president and chief operating officer of The Stop & Shop Companies, you have to learn that rejection doesn't mean personal failure.

At the age of fifteen, Goldberg recalls, she was excluded from a local girls' club. "It was painful," she remembers, "although it was just a neighborhood group, but it was significant because it established the idea that frustration can be a constructive learning experience."

Carol Goldberg today is the CEO of the thirteenth largest supermarket chain in the United States, and is also active in countless projects ranging from the Boston Symphony to the Task Force on Future Planning of the U.S. Office of Education. She still believes that early rejection was the single most important event contributing to her success.

⬤ Don't overlook the little things.

Carelessness with details sinks more careers than anyone will admit.

Watch yourself so you adhere to the nitty-gritty demands of the job. (Are they bugged when you arrive at 8:04 instead of 8:00? Do they mean it when they say they want desk tops left perfectly clean at night?)

⬤ Don't talk too much in large meetings.

Best answer when asked a direct question you prefer not to answer at that moment is, "I'd like to think about that and get back to you."

Then make sure you do both.

⬤ Always say yes.

Because nothing ever happens to women who say no.

▄ Make yourself known for same-day response.

If you get a request for information, respond on the same day with a memo reporting the information or the date when you will have it. In other words, always let people know not only that they have been heard but that their words inspire action. Speed and courtesy are two attributes of a promotable person.

▄ Establish your credibility early in the game.

If you're going to get ahead in any business—and more particularly, if it is a business that is male-dominated—make sure that you are regarded as energetic, serious, and tough.

That's what Marjorie Weber, a partner in Florida Fidelity Financial, one of her state's biggest mortgage brokers specializing in commercial real estate, learned.

"To establish my credibility, I made sure I had good relationships in business, particularly with my peer group, and I continued educating myself. I took courses. I had credentials. Long ago I went for my MAI." (Member of the American Institute, the recognized appraisal group.)

"But," says Weber somewhat ruefully, "let's face it. The older you get in this business, the more respect you get. And that's true even for men. The big real estate developers working with millions and millions of dollars don't want to think they're dealing with kids."

≣ Don't brood over mistakes.

Sure, some things will go wrong. Smooth them as best you can, and move to the next major event. Nothing good happens if you keep moaning about the past.

≣ Take a computer course.

Most people over 24 don't know a microchip from software. You're an instant authority when you prove you can talk the language. Besides, why be outprogrammed by a disc-cluster-system-spouting 22-year-old?

As you keep moving up, more and more decisions center around the computer: Which model should we buy? Are our computers really obsolete? Do we need more programmers? Does the San Antonio office need a computer room?

These are capital decisions that must be made with knowledge. If you have to depend on opinions without information of your own, you will become a victim of the Corporate Computer Wars.

€ **Look up every word you come across that you can't define (e.g., animus, crepitate, recension).**

And do it now.

€ **Do the part of the job you like least first.**

Then you have the good stuff ahead of you, and your own enthusiasm will give you the ideas and energy for the best part of the assignment.

€ **Divide to conquer.**

No job looks too complex if you reduce it to a single action—which is then followed by another action. And another. Until the job is done.

✇ Learn to survive in order to succeed.

No woman who has survived and succeeded was ever put to the test more dramatically than Marilyn MacGruder Barnewall, now one of the most successful bankers in America.

Back in 1961 her husband was sent to prison as the result of a messy police department scandal. She had two babies, three months and eighteen months old. She had been in an automobile accident and needed surgery, and she was on welfare.

Today her company, bearing her name, is headquartered in Denver and serves as consultant on profitability analysis to banks throughout the United States, Europe, and Australia, as well as Russia and China.

"How did I do it? Out of desperation," she says in answer to her own question. "When I was on welfare, what I saw was such a different scenario from what I had known. You create your own reality by the picture you have of yourself. The people on welfare had no respect for others because they had no self-respect.

"I was determined to have self-respect. I got a job as a legal secretary and said I took shorthand. I didn't, but I managed to work out my own code because I needed a job. Later I went back to school, and ultimately earned my graduate degree from the University of Colorado. I became the first female vice-president of the United Bank of Denver.

"But before that came the plan for survival—job, operation, care for the children. After I figured how to survive, I was able to engineer the ways to succeed."

≡ Don't be afraid to ask successful people for advice.

You don't have to wait for formal networking.

In 1961 Nina Blanchard took $300 ($100 for a desk, $200 for a license) and decided to start a model agency in California. She came to New York to try to plug into the business there. Two people were instantly helpful: Eileen Ford and Ali McGraw. Eileen Ford, the owner of the successful Ford agency, showed Nina her booking cards and explained systems; Ali McGraw, then employed by photographer Mel Sokolsky, was also willing to show Nina the way New York worked with models. Today the Ford agency and the Blanchard agency collaborate often; the two women are dear friends, and Ali McGraw still calls Nina Blanchard when she sees someone she thinks has a future in the business.

All of this happened because Blanchard, a novice, had the courage to approach the top people in the profession she wanted to enter—and because she realized that her success would also help their businesses.

≡ Hang around after office hours.

That's the best time to see the boss (or any superior), and chances are that not only is he or she more relaxed but you'll be remembered as the person who cares enough to stay late and is interested enough to learn more.

≋ Be tougher on yourself than anybody else would be.

If you get an assignment today, and it's due next week or next month or next year, start it today. And finish it as soon as possible. Always get work done before the deadline so that you have the luxury of making changes.

≋ Don't ever take advice from anyone who starts a sentence with, "You may not like me for this, but it's for your own good—"

It never is.

≋ If you don't respect the company you are working for, get out.

Don't think you can change things.

You can't change a company any more than you can change a husband.

◀ Take time to take time.

Don't come in and announce that you had four vacation days you never took. Unspent vacation time isn't appreciated by your company; no modern manager wants to be Simon Legree (and if you find one who does, you'd better leave that company fast).

And do take care of yourself. When you're sick or overtired, ambition is the first thing to go.

◀ Join trade associations and women's networking groups.

Forget all about that speech you made when you told friends you weren't a joiner.

Who says you can't change your mind—especially if changing offers you the opportunity to learn about your business and share your experiences with those who will understand you best: other women who work and have similar problems and frustrations.

A universal advantage of networking is that it gives you the female point of view, often from women outside your industry. Networking can sometimes lead to your next job. Isabel Leeds became Public Affairs Director of WMCA-Radio because she met the station owner through the Women's Forum, an executive women's group in New York.

☙ Look for mentors both inside and outside your company.

Identify the people in your company and industry whom you respect, then volunteer your time and effort in order to work with them, listen to them, or be associated with them.

So long as you expect a mentor to serve primarily as a role model and not as your personal guru, you won't be disappointed. And if you seek advice and opinions from your mentor about your industry generally—and not your own career—you'll help your career even more.

☙ Don't rush the clock.

Most six-figure women agree with June M. Collier, the president and CEO of National Industries, Inc., in Montgomery, Alabama, who says, "My success has been slow and steady with hard work and hard decisions."

Collier, whose company's interests include such things as the manufacture of wiring harnesses for automotive, appliance, and aerospace needs and manual automotive antennas, was graduated from high school at the age of sixteen. In 1961 she joined Mid-South Electrical Fabricators, Inc., of Jackson, Mississippi, and stayed with the company as it grew and changed to its present form and size ($40 million in 1982).

"I started with various clerical and lower management positions," she says, "and I had luck. But it all took time."

Practice your big moments in front of a mirror.

If you want to know how you'll look asking for a raise, making a presentation, or selling your basic philosophy, there's just one way to find out.

Act promotable.

Don't let anyone think you work because you have to.

If something's worth crying about, go ahead and cry.

But don't make tears a regular part of your act.

It's kind of funny, but now that we think it's all right for men to cry, we're horrified when women do.

But, life being what it is, there are things to cry about. And sometimes they happen at work.

∉ Don't do cozy little dinners with your male associates and their spouses.

Of course we're all liberated.

Of course we're all crazy about each other.

But his wife doesn't want to know that you know that much about him. And your spouse isn't too wild about the whole thing either.

∉ Don't flaunt your eccentricities: nobody trusts a weirdo.

In my business we've had more flakes than Kellogg's.

We once had an art director who tossed Pentel pens at the ceiling because he liked the pretty dots over his head.

We had one man who ran down our long corridor, slid under the receptionist's desk and screamed, "Safe!"

We had a secretary who was in love with the audio-visual equipment and locked herself in the studio for hours at a time.

A bookkeeper once set our record for late-to-work excuses. She would arrive at 2 P.M. with reasons that ranged from "I cut my legs while shaving, and the bleeding wouldn't stop" to "My cat shut off the alarm and I just woke up."

You have to be an established star in your business before eccentric or unconventional behavior is tolerated.

⬤ Learn to accept criticism.

Never respond with, "Yes, but…"

Ask instead, "How can I do it (make it) (see it) better?"

⬤ If you've been fired, don't resign from the world.

The firing probably didn't come as a surprise, but the timing did. You thought you had more time. You thought that you could say goodbye and do it your way.

But today someone said, "Your department is overstaffed," or, "This hasn't worked out the way we thought it would." Doesn't matter exactly what was said. All that matters is that it was said, and you're back on the street.

What do you do first?

Ask for time. If you can hold on to the desk and the phone for a couple of weeks, you'll be in the position of someone who has a job and is looking. And that's always a better view.

If the answer is no, then see if a relative or friend will permit you to use an office number for your calls.

And if none of that works, head for home and start the campaign for the next job. Call all the people who have worked with you (not at the old office, but in other offices), and explain that you're looking. Call all close friends, and tell them you're available for a new job— do they know about anything?

Write to all the people you'd like to work for. And write to them by name. I get a lot of letters every year addressed to "Dear Sir." Those are the ones I never answer.

Read the newspapers; find articles about companies that sound interesting, and send the clipping together with a personal letter to the chief executive officer telling why you like what you read and what you have to offer that company.

Read the want ads. And if none of this works, see a first-rate employment agency. How do you find one? Ask an executive in the field that interests you. Even though his or her company may not use recruiters, executives always know the good ones for their business.

And once you start going for interviews, say nothing nasty about the company or person who fired you. No one wants to hire a bad-mouthing complainer.

◧ Be the best fire-fighter on the block.

Promotions go to people who can save the business that's going out the door.

The better you are at spotting smoke signals and keeping fires from erupting, the fatter will be your paycheck and the quicker your climb.

☯ Take credit when it's deserved.

And never when it isn't.

☯ Recognize that you're human, too.

It is possible to love your children and guide their growth even if you don't stand there with milk and cookies as they come trudging home from school. (It's definitely possible, but no one except another working mother will believe you).

It is possible to work all day and then go out at night without falling asleep during the movie, concert, or play. (However, I have never met anyone who could do this three nights in a row.)

It is possible to live on your present salary and save money while you dress like someone on the best-dressed list, eat at the best restaurants, and enjoy all popular entertainments. (However, no one has ever done it.)

⬤ Nobody's broke so long as she has talent and ingenuity.

Peggy Vandervoort was running a multimillion-dollar racing stable and breeding operation in Florida ten years ago when she suddenly found her considerable personal assets tied up in a divorce action.

"I literally had my present career kicked off by my divorce," she said. "Here I was, a known horse breeder, with no horses to breed. I just couldn't afford to buy horses. What to do?

"I realized I'd have to start a different way. One thing you learn during a divorce is that you can't lie down and die. You just have to figure out how to make money in a new way. So I did.

"I became an international consultant to breeders and owners. Then I branched out and became bigger than I'd ever been before. I started limited partnerships, bought horses and managed the investments. Then I went still further and created tax shelters—syndicated limited partnerships.

"I got into areas I didn't dare enter before. I think that's true of a lot of us women. We can do more—but we wait until we're pushed."

€ **When you set your long-range goals, look all the way to the top.**

Where you want to go will have a lot to do with how you get there.

M. L. Sirianni, now a management consultant running her own company in Los Angeles, was formerly senior director of marketing for Max Factor, and prior to that had profit responsibilities for businesses worth more than 100 million dollars at H. J. Heinz, Playtex, and Clairol.

"I spent more than five years struggling up the ladder of Fortune 500 marketing companies," she recalls, "before I looked ahead to the president's job. And by the time I did, I knew I didn't want that job ultimately. As a result my desire for the autonomy of my own business blossomed."

€ **Before you look for your next job, make sure you've mastered this one.**

☙ Spot your next job—and go for it.

It may be in your present company, then again it may not.

☙ Ask for your next job from the company's point of view.

If you want to advance in your present company, remember that no president wants to make you a vice-president because (1) your boyfriend or spouse thinks you should be one; (2) everybody else is; or (3) you think it's about time.

What very few of us who run companies ever find is a person (male or female) who comes in for review and says, "I think I know how *we* [not *I*] can make more money," and then proceeds to detail how the company will profit by raising either her pay or status.

Where, oh where, are the people for the next level of management who will come forward and tell us why elevating them is good for business?

If you interview at a new company, know something about the company and where your talents fit. Instead of just asking for a job, *show* how your skills and experience may fit their needs.

≋ Avoid lateral moves.

There are no absolutes about job changing. There is no rule that says you must spend one year at a job before moving on. But you should beware of too many switches on your résumé. Frequent musical chairs in your career mean either (1) you're never satisfied or (2) your employer is never satisfied.

One way to keep from making wrong moves is to ask yourself these questions before you accept a new position:

1. Does it pay more?
2. Does it offer more responsibility?
3. Does it make it possible for me to move up faster?
4. Is the competition for the next level beatable? (In other words, are there few people at the next level who are my age? Have my background? Have my talents?)
5. Do I like this company well enough to want to advance in it?
6. Are the working conditions either as good as or better than those where I now work?
7. Do they have a wholesome, constructive attitude toward women?
8. Am I going to learn something new and/or will this job sharpen my talents and make me better?

If you have at least five yes answers, take a deep breath and go for it.

But if you come up with five no answers, just keep doing what you're doing and wait for a better offer at a better time.

II

$25,000 TO $75,000: THE MIDDLE GROUND

You have passed the first hurdle, and now you are on your way.

You are probably in marketing, finance, or have a profession (law, medicine).

You are not yet 40 years old, may or may not be married.

When you first went to work, you didn't think you would hold the job you have today. Your willingness to change, your flexibility are key factors in your present success.

You work more than 40 hours a week, spend as much as one-fifth of your work time on business trips away from the office.

You are not a member of a corporate board of directors, but probably serve on a number of volunteer advisory boards in the arts and social services.

Along with earning $25,000 you have also earned a title; perhaps it is an assistant vice-presidency. You now have a secretary and possibly one other person reporting to you.

Many people are watching you. It is generally accepted that you are a candidate for the next generation of management, and this is the crossroads of your business life. You are balanced precariously (in business all balance is precarious) between promotion and exit. One of the first things we all learn in business is that we must grow: we grow up or we grow out.

So you are poised for flight—up or out.

If you choose to stay, then your life will center around your ability to sharpen your talents, your ability to create opportunities that will permit you to flower, your ability to answer the challenge of increased responsibility.

The traps, and there are traps, lie in the increasing competition from both men and women; the difficulty in getting management to properly evaluate your still-developing skills in order to avoid the wasteland of dead-end jobs; and the need to push aside the battle fatigue that comes from the pressures both inside and outside the office.

You are accepting a risk as you climb because inability to perform can result in job termination—firing—and subsequent loss of both public and self-esteem.

In the face of this kind of stress, now is the time to assess your own desires and consider the rewards of success. Just what is it that success will bring?

You look better.

A man I know once saw an acquaintance after she got her first promotion. She was chic, lovely-looking. He looked at her and said, "Success has gone to your face." Women, even more than men, radiate from the center, and when we are satisfied with ourselves and our accomplishments, it shows in our faces. There is less visible stress. We are more likely to have our bodies in shape. No neglect to skin or hair. Successful women have a professional look, a look that communicates to others, "This is the best I can be."

You have access to more people.

Your circle widens as you move up in business, and the closer you get to the top, the more interesting the cast becomes. As your authority and responsibilities broaden, more people will seek you out. You will find you can schedule luncheon dates outside your own business, invite a larger spectrum of talented people to your home. What all this does, of course, is open doors so that—

You have a more interesting and satisfying life, with increased intellectual stimulation.

As you climb the power levels of business, you will travel more. You will also have the opportunity to further educate yourself—seminars, special courses. More of the world will be accessible to you so that your own opportunities for personal growth will increase enormously.

You have freedom and the luxuries increased money and position bring.

You never have complete freedom, but there is a kind of freedom that comes when you have cars (your own or leased), cabs, or limos at your disposal. There is freedom that comes when you can afford household help to clean, cook, and supervise children during your workday. You have freedom from guilt when you can help people in your life who need an extra boost (either financial or psychological). There is freedom in having more privacy (no more six-across flights) and more space (bigger apartment, more acreage, fewer neighbors). You have better art, pretty clothes, the ability to give your children the kind of education they need. And life is— well, comfortable. A woman in the communications industry said, "Being a working woman meant I never had to do all those things I hate. I didn't have to be a mother. I didn't have to to country clubs. I didn't have to get married unless I wanted to. People say working puts a woman in a competitive world; I always thought *not* working was much harder."

Another reported, "It made me special. Because I was successful in this area of life, I didn't have to be as beautiful, didn't have to be as good a tennis player, didn't have to compete at the prom level where most of my friends were."

Again and again women tell of seeking refuge, a

private world where, despite the rules and regulations of business, they were free of the rules and regulations of the traditionally oriented woman.

One thing works in reverse, however, for successful women. As salaries climb, the choice of men narrows. Money and position are only the outward reasons. The more you accomplish in business, the more men appear to be threatened. Successful women don't always respect men who are less successful than they.

There are few instances where marriages between women and men less visible than their wives work well. Not many men can play second fiddle to high-flying corporate wives.

This is also the time you will ask the basic questions of life and career: Is it worth it? Should I marry? Is this what I want my life to be? Should I have more children? Should I spend more time with the child I have? Should I divorce?

In the background of all this is the ticking of the biological time-clock. It isn't fair. Men can have children until they no longer walk the face of the earth. But there's a time limit for women, so there must be a choice.

There are business choices too. Now is the time you will wonder, "Should I go into my own business?"

Carolyn Doppelt Gray, an official of the U.S. Small Business Administration, says, as quoted in *The Wall Street Journal*, "The 1970s was the decade of women entering management, and the 1980s is turning out to be the decade of the woman entrepreneur."

Further, The Small Business Administration reports that the number of self-employed women increased 35 percent from 1977 to 1982. During the same period the number of self-employed men increased 12 percent. Women own businesses that today account for more than $40 billion in annual revenues.

But while the early women entrepreneurs included those running the traditional kinds of women's businesses

(Elizabeth Arden, Helena Rubinstein, Estée Lauder, Anne Klein), the new woman entrepreneur is making her way in the general business world of finance, manufacturing, construction, and—increasingly—computers.

Generally the woman who goes out on her own has previous business experience in the field; sometimes her own business provides the opportunity for growth and advancement denied when she works for another company. The entrepreneur is often a woman who has taken time off for child-raising and returns with her own company in a role that rewards her years at home; many times she is aided both financially and emotionally by the husband she helped in previous years.

As you start your climb through the middle ground, here are some of the experiences and the advice of women who have been there.

℮ Relax! The panic will subside in about sixty days.

These are the "oh-my-God-I-don't-think-I-can-do-it" days of a new assignment.

All of a sudden you think there is more information than you can ever absorb, more systems than you can manage, more politics than you anticipated, more interruptions than you can handle, more expectations than you can live up to.

But stop for a few minutes. Look around you. Those people who are your peers aren't smarter, better qualified, or in possession of more hours a day than you. They did it, and so will you. And if it's any comfort, one thing that most women are finding is that once they reach senior status, the people around them aren't really *that* smart.

So these first months, slow down, take your time, and you'll find you can handle everything from the rotten first assistant to the unbearable deadlines with more aplomb than you first thought.

℮ Don't tell everyone how to do things until you've been on the job 90 days.

For the first 90 days, speak softly and carry a big pencil, so you can write down all your suggestions and then decide which ones are worth voicing 90 days later.

● Make sure you say "we" when you talk about the company.

"They" are not they anymore.

They are we. And we are the future of the company. That means that, as a person running the company, you are aligned with management and responsible for what happens today and tomorrow.

That female part of us is willing to take responsibility for today, but many of us do not see ourselves as the future.

But we are. Consider the alternative.

● Don't go too far with your new authority.

Management is not a precise science. The pressures a CEO applies do not work in the same way as the pressures *you* apply as a divisional merchandise manager.

Management is as dependent on *who* says what and does it as it is on what is said and done. So don't waste your time deciding how you'd handle each of your CEO's moves. By the time you get there, the social and economic climate will be different. And so will you.

◉ Learn all the new names as quickly as possible.

One of the best ways to learn the new names is to write them individually on file cards. Don't have your secretary do it; this is one thing you ought to do yourself, for as you write the name you will begin to remember it.

After you meet each person, write one (or two) things that will help you remember him or her. Did you once work in the same office? Do you share an enthusiasm for pasta or ballet?

Then, before your meetings, always try to get a list of those who will be in attendance; review your cards, and you'll be amazed how much easier you'll find name recall.

◉ Learn to play golf.

Or bridge. Or tennis. Or whatever game it is that the bosses in your company play.

It's important to go where the power gathers.

In a recent survey of Harvard Business School graduates, most attributed success to two factors: luck and the people they knew. Remember, you don't meet many people sitting at home.

There are a lot of deals made at a lot of golf clubs in this country, and one of the big problems of women has been the fact that we don't get to see men in that relaxed atmosphere.

☰ Find your restaurants.

Recognize that women still have a long way to go in getting the attention of captains, headwaiters, and restaurant owners.

Find one or two restaurants near your office. Introduce yourself to the owner, and tell him or her that you want to use the restaurant frequently for business lunches. Choose a table that is somewhat private, conducive to good talk, and explain that whenever possible (and on adequate notice) you want that table held for you.

Set up a charge account with a fixed amount (fifteen to twenty percent) automatically added to your bill, and agree that a check will never be presented to you at the table.

It's all more gracious, more hospitable—and, most of all, more professional.

≋ Program your lunches.

Lunch can be the best part of the day if you use it to meet people in your business, see friends you can't see at other times, go to museums, exercise, or get to know someone in your office a little better.

Don't leave lunches to chance.

At the beginning of each month, look at your calendar, find some open dates, and telephone some of the people you've meant to call. You'll find you will get to know them. It's flattering to be asked to lunch; people rarely say no. And there is nothing like a business lunch in an appropriate restaurant (not too glitzy, not a fast-food emporium) to establish excellent feelings of friendship that can lead to valuable networking.

≋ Learn one job well because you can then do any job well.

"Every occupation is the same because it requires concentration, perfectionism, and interest," says Phyllis Cerf Wagner.

Wagner, plucked from her Oklahoma home at the age of 15 by her cousin Ginger Rogers, went to California where she was discovered by David O. Selznick and became a contract player at RKO.

"I hated the picture business," she recalls, "but I did make lifelong friends like Betty Furness. I went to

MacFadden Publishing and wrote a column called "The Hollywood Young Stars," then did some feature articles for *Photoplay*. That led to a job offer at McCann-Erickson, the New York advertising agency, and at the age of 20 I worked in their radio department and eventually became a producer of daytime soap operas."

Along the way she met Random House publisher Bennett Cerf, whom she married. "Bennett always said one must never waste a good mind, so I worked until our son Christopher was born. Then I became involved in charities during the war years. But my friend Alicia Patterson insisted I work for a living, so I wrote a column for her newspaper called 'What's New?' That led to a column for *Good Housekeeping*, doing cryptograms for *The Saturday Review*, and eventually, by virtue of my own concerns that I expressed to Bennett, a role in developing children's books at Random House." Later she did a series of exercise books with Marjorie Craig.

Now a vice-president at Wells, Rich, Greene, the advertising agency, Phyllis Cerf Wagner is part of her agency's new business team and civic task force. "I always maintained my interest in charities," she asserts, "because I think it is important to have hospitals and scholarships that are privately funded."

A gracious and charming hostess, she married Mayor Robert Wagner several years after the death of Cerf. "I haven't had any difficulty moving from place to place," she claims, "because if you understand concepts, you can do anything. The basic concepts, regardless of job description, are to do adequate research, perform the work on time, and be as accurate as possible."

⬤ Get friendly on the phone with the secretaries of people you call, and be your own telephone operator.

Make your own calls, and answer your own phones. There is nothing more frustrating than to pick up your phone and hear a secretary ask you to hold for Mr. So-and-So, then wait until he is ready to take your call. It's frequently a he. Women are usually more courteous than that.

The advantage of making your own calls is that secretaries can help you reach the person you want, give you information about his or her availability and—because secretaries give messages in any order they choose—a secretary just may arrange to get your message on top of the pile.

⬤ Make decisions promptly.

Honestly, it's better to make a wrong decision than to make no decision at all.

Obviously, too many wrong decisions will eventually catch up with you and get you in trouble, but no decisions will frustrate everyone—above and below—who works with you.

The faster you make decisions, the better you demonstrate your ability to handle responsibility and authority.

● Assess your talents, and look for ways to stretch them.

When Ann Piestrup founded The Learning Company, the computer software company for children's learning in Menlo Park, California, she was an experienced teacher, mother, and researcher. But she was no businesswoman.

"But with background and the desire to improve learning opportunities for children, I set out to learn what I needed to know, to find people to help—the best people in the business. When I began, I didn't know about computers, accounting, taxes, or other business matters."

Yet learn she did, and along the way she persuaded people she respected—venture capitalists, government agencies and an industry foundation—to help her follow her vision, and raised $300,000 in venture capital.

"I realized that the microcomputer could transform educational opportunities for children," she says, "and I am very proud that my six-year-old daughter can see her mother in a productive, rewarding role."

A former member of the Order of the Sisters of St. Joseph, Piestrup now serves as chairman of The Learning Company in Menlo Park, California.

▰ Always make sure you're talking to someone who can say yes.

All corporations are filled with levels of people who can say no.

When we first presented the line, "With a name like Smucker's it has to be good," all the people in the room looked nervously at Paul Smucker. No one said anything. Finally one man spoke. "If we run that line, we'll be out of business in six months." Three others nodded in agreement.

Still Paul Smucker said nothing. Finally he asked the agency, "Do you think it will sell jelly?"

We assured him we believed it would.

Finally Paul spoke. "Let's run it."

And that's what business is all about: one person who can say yes.

▰ Become famous for your short meetings.

Long meetings thwart high-level productivity. Besides, long meetings are boring. Once I attended a meeting that dealt with a plant budget report. (Advertising is not all shoots on Capri and sittings with Avedon.) The assistant treasurer droned on and on. Finally the chairman, realizing that attention was not riveted on the still-talking officer, said, "And in conclusion?"

"I'm not finished," the assistant treasurer said as he kept talking.

Wrong. A week later he was quite finished.

To control and shorten meeting times, always distribute an agenda prior to the meeting with an indication of the time allotted to each subject. With this document in hand, you are always able to move to the next topic because of time pressures.

In addition, be certain that someone is assigned to write the minutes of the meeting and that they are distributed only to those people who need to be informed of the decisions made. Don't send minutes to every person in a department when one copy that can be circulated among them will do. Don't create paper snowstorms and lines at the Xerox machine in the name of "communications."

And about those meetings—if you can keep most of yours to less than fifteen minutes, you are certain to earn Brownie points.

€ Stay lean but not mean; tough but not rough.

Remember your last job and how much you appreciated people who explained things to you? If so, then help others now.

You don't have to become a junior Ann Landers. You don't have to sniffle over each broken romance in your department to prove you're empathetic, but it's just human to show concern over major problems affecting the lives and subsequent performance of associates.

Do not, however, permit employees to make your office the Corporate Wailing Wall.

☰ Don't be afraid to go for the big one.

It is always easier to make a sale to a rich and powerful company (or individual) than a small, underfinanced one. The people with the smallest budgets always have the biggest opinions.

Our agency once had 40 smallish clients, and each one of them agonized over every comma and apostrophe in the advertising. We began to grow when we approached the bigger companies and dealt with those executives who really wanted to be counseled and knew they needed advice.

What I've learned is that people who run good-sized businesses know they must depend on outside counsel and so are willing to accept it in every area—legal, financial, real estate, taxes, advertising.

There is also a corollary to this:

☰ Don't try to sell a $19.95 dress to a $199.95 customer.

Nobody's ever offended if you show him something beyond his reach.

◉ When it comes to originality, proceed with caution.

Most companies say they want original thinking, but they buy conformity, that corporate comfort.

Early on you have to decide whether you want to give people what they say they want—or what makes them comfortable.

There are five questions to ask yourself before presenting an original idea:

1. Is the idea affordable under present budgeting?
2. Does the idea fit the chairman's or president's view of the corporate posture?
3. Can the idea be executed by present management?
4. Will the idea reflect well on your superiors, as well as on you?
5. Is it something you will be assigned so that you have the opportunity to shepherd it personally?

If you can answer "yes" to three of the five questions, it's probably worth pursuing—and presenting.

◉ After you take a firm stand on an issue, don't be afraid to change positions.

And don't be afraid to say you were wrong.

It's the sign of a working mind, and no boss ever complained about a working mind.

● Separate your own ego from your business ego.

"The very first time I went out to sell advertising space for my magazine, *Avenue*, I called the head of one of the biggest agencies in the world," recalls Judith Price.

"When he answered the phone and I told him what I wanted, he launched into a tirade and used an obscenity that I'd never even heard before. I was so shaken that I hung up, burst into tears, and called my husband.

"He listened to my story and then asked, 'Do you believe in your magazine? Do you want to get advertisers? Do you really want this?' I answered yes to all his questions, and he gave me the best advice anyone ever gave me. He said that I'd never be successful in business if I assumed that every negative thing was said about *me*, Judy. That agency president was talking about salespeople; that was his attitude toward them. I was still exactly the same woman I was before I made that call.

"I dried my eyes, went ahead and tried to sell more ads."

Indeed Price did sell more ads. *Avenue*, the magazine she founded and publishes, is now sold in New York, Houston, Dallas, Chicago, Los Angeles, San Francisco, and Palm Beach.

● Don't be supercilious.

Nobody cares about your present success—except you, your mom, and the person trying to replace you.

● It isn't fair.

No matter what anyone tells you about persons who are thrifty, brave, and reverent reaping all the rewards, remember that it's just not so.

Business, all business, is at one time or another exciting, overwhelming, tiring, interesting, fascinating, absorbing, exhilarating, joyous, a drag, thrilling, dazzling, preoccupying and boring.

But it's not always fair. And no one can promise you that it will be.

You will work very hard on a project, then watch someone else waltz off with the credit, recognition, and financial rewards.

You will ingratiate yourself and your company, totally charm someone... only to see the business go down the street.

You will give the best service and make the best product; then someone up there will make the wrong decision, and all your good effort will go for naught.

You will reward someone with your loyalty, your devotion, and your best work; then that someone will reward someone else with the promotion or order that you expected.

No. It's not fair. But what keeps us all going is that it *is* exciting, overwhelming, etcetera.

☰ Always look rich.

And the best way to look rich (if you're not) is to wear inexpensive, understated clothes—and very expensive accessories. The best color for looking rich: black.

☰ Know the market.

We once had a client who made bagels. You know. Bagels. As in lox and cream cheese.

One day our bagel client decided to expand beyond New York and go to Indiana. We ran a super ad for them in the Fort Wayne newspaper.

The headline said FREE BAGELS. But the ad didn't pull. You see, in Fort Wayne, Indiana, no one knew what a bagel was.

So before you astound the world with your cleverness and creativity, make sure you've done the appropriate market research.

☻ Aim often, but fire infrequently.

You can't run any business if you cry "Wolf," but on the other hand, you must let people know that there are standards to be met, rules to be followed.

Generally a word of warning will cause the troops to shape up. But nothing gets an office working more like an office than the knowledge that you can—and will—fire someone who is not performing.

☻ Always hire people who are better than you.

Hiring dummies is shortsighted.

You can't move up the ladder until everyone is comfortable with your replacement.

▄ Invest in yourself.

Clothes, vacations, and homes are not luxuries. They are investments because they make you a more valuable asset.

Faith Stewart-Gordon, the president of the Russian Tea Room in New York, believes that as a woman becomes more successful she ought to bring more fun to her life, increase her sense of well-being, and fight the pressures with physical and mental stretching.

▄ Keep the office aware of your comings and goings.

Your secretary (or whoever answers phones at the office for you) should know always where you are, how to reach you, and which calls must be forwarded immediately.

It is far more professional for a caller to hear, "She will be back in the office in forty-five minutes," than to have a secretary say, "I think she'll be back sometime this afternoon."

☰ All work leads somewhere.

Writer and television interviewer/producer Barbaralee Diamonstein's longtime involvement in the arts, architecture, and public service inspired her to write a book about adaptive reuse of older structures. While Diamonstein was in the midst of her writing, the editor who was shepherding the project left her job and requested that Diamonstein take the book to the editor's next publisher.

Diamonstein agreed, but ten months later the editor had no job, so that meant Diamonstein had no publisher. What to do?

"Keep working," said Barbaralee Diamonstein. So, with limited funds and the devotion of her small staff, the research and writing continued. Eventually her work came to the attention of Cass Canfield, Jr., at Harper & Row, and he agreed to publish *Buildings Reborn: New Uses, Old Places*.

Now, six years later, the book is an increasingly important text for design and planning students and professionals.

€ Look for the positive to be found in every negative action.

Betty Ruth Hollander is chairman and CEO of The Omega Group, a high-tech electronics company employing 500 people. She eschews the private office, sits in a big room with others. "I get lonely," explains the mother of four who began her business out of her home in 1962.

"Success is a state of mind," believes Hollander. "You can take every difficult thing and turn it around to work in your favor. When this business began, the world was so sexist that I couldn't get an accountant or a bank officer to talk to me unless my husband was in the room. By 1968, however, we'd grown enough so that some investment bankers considered taking us public.

"They brought in outside financial people who went so far as to suggest that my husband leave his job and join Omega so that the prospectus would look good. Financial people felt my credentials wouldn't sell stock."

Fortunately those fears caused them to turn down the opportunity to take Omega public. Betty Ruth Hollander now considers that turndown the single most important event that contributed to the company's success. "We went on to do it our way," she explains.

She is also quick to credit her husband's encouragement, guidance, and patience—and to point out that while some men had difficulty adjusting to women in business, others were found (including her first landlord) who were trusting and helpful.

● Never give all the reasons why something can't be done.

Anyone can do that. And, as chairman Edward Jefferson of Du Pont said, "It's a characteristic of life that the crepehangers talk louder than those who have the will to get things done."

● Find a good mentor.

A good mentor is one who

1. Urges you to expand your company contacts beyond him (or her);
2. Never tells you what to do but instead advises on ways to make your decision;
3. Points out corporate dangers but doesn't gossip;
4. Shows you how to find answers but doesn't spoon-feed information to you.

● Acknowledge the help you get.

That's the only way you'll get it again.

Sandra Meyer, president of the Communications Division of the American Express Company, thanks Ralph Cobb, the executive who promoted her to Senior Product Manager at General Foods and the person who helped her most in her career.

Leda Sanford, who has been the publisher of several magazines, believes the single most important event in her business life occurred when publisher/editor John Mack Carter recommended her to Raymond K. Mason, at that time the owner of *American Home*. Mason then made her a publisher in his company.

Both agree that the good manners of a public thank you make good business sense.

● When two people in the office disagree, stay out of the fight.

I once tried to mediate a difference of opinion between two co-workers. In the end they found they really liked each other—it was me they couldn't stand. I lost their friendship, and eventually they both left the agency.

● Don't out-macho the men.

Watch what you say and the ways you say it.

Watch the ways you decide to display the new kind of woman you are. At a meeting of executive women, a young woman stood up to speak, and out of the mouth of this attractive, bright, interesting female came that ultimate four-letter word—not once, but again and again.

So what did she prove? Only that she was able to irritate older women, embarrass younger ones, and cause everyone to question her sense and sensibility. We women are still the new kids on the block. We don't have to go out and break arms to prove that we're tough and competent.

● Don't follow the crowd.

When everybody else is standing up, sit down. When they jump, stand still.

☀ Release, refresh, relax, return.

That's the formula for easing tension.

Release the tension, refresh and relax the body—and then return to work.

These tension relievers (they're not exercises) will release at-the-desk fatigue. They were developed by Marcia Lesser-Carpenter, a psychomotor therapist, who concentrates on stress-related physical problems.

A. *Deep Breathing*

Sit back in your chair, and close your eyes and mouth. Inhale through your nose for two counts, hold the breath for four counts, then exhale and "stay empty" for two counts. Repeat five times.

B. *Eye Movement*

Hold each of the following actions for three counts: look 1) up, 2) down, 3) side right, 4) side left, 5) high diagonally, both sides, 6) low diagonally, both sides. Close eyes, relax, then repeat two times.

C. *Mouth and Jaw Movement*

Pucker the lips; open mouth as wide as possible—as if to scream. Repeat five times.

D. *Feet*

Take off your shoes, and rotate the ankles ten times in each direction.

E. *Standing*

Stand shoeless, and with feet six inches apart (all movements should be almost imperceptible):

1. Move head in circular motion as slowly as possible; make the center of the top of your head the source of movement; repeat five times.

2. Move shoulders and rib cage only in a circular motion like a very slow hula. Concentrate on your middle back and back shoulder area; reverse; do very slow movements.

3. Next, move only pelvic area—circle hips in a very slow hula.

4. Concentrate on the entire spine from tailbone to the middle of the head, and combine all of the movements above. *The key is to feel like a top spinning in slow motion.* Let go of any tension by concentrating on that particular area and relaxing. Move six times in each direction.
5. Remain standing, feeling calm, your spine stretched and long.
6. Take two deep breaths—and back to the business at hand.

◉ Be supportive of men.

If he is over 30, he was raised to believe that even though little girls might be smarter in school, big men would grow up to get it all. But now men watch as we fill the law and medical schools, and they have to stand by while some of us take jobs they expected to have. I don't think women should give back any of the jobs and education; I just think women should practice being gracious winners.

 ● **Don't be afraid to add some humor, particularly when you're the only woman in the group.**

"A little shared laughter can make everyone more comfortable, get rid of underlying tensions, and so make a meeting progress faster," says Jane Evans, the executive vice president of the $650 million General Mills fashion apparel and accessories division.

Evans, an early addition to America's corporate suites (she was president of I. Miller at the age of 25) is often the only woman in a meeting and is known for her marketing skills and people talents.

"Humor," she warns, "should never be directed at another person, and it is equally important not to make yourself the center of the laughter. The idea is to focus humor on the problem, so that you can quickly create an atmosphere that is both relaxed and businesslike."

⬤ Don't fall in love on company time.

It changes the balance of working relationships and creates unwelcome personal tensions. If you do develop a special relationship within the company, one of you should make plans to find another job.

For every Mary Cunningham (whose highly publicized alleged romance led to a new executive position) there are thousands of women looking for jobs.

⬤ Don't play all your cards at once.

Maintain a little mystery, and apply the things you know as a woman to the things you do as an executive. Barbara Howar, the writer and TV personality, tells the story of the time she wanted to meet Henry Kissinger, then single and the catch of Washington. Mrs. Howar persuaded a friend to invite her to dinner and seat her next to Mr. Kissinger. Halfway through the dinner Mr. Kissinger turned to Mrs. Howar and said, "Perhaps we can have dinner one night." Mrs. Howar, eager and anxious, replied, "Anything you want." Said Mr. Kissinger, "Dinner will be quite enough."

Moral: Never give more than the buyer asks.

☙ Forget about being named Miss Congeniality.

Women on the way up generally fail to win popularity contests.

The only compensation is that once you're there you will become very well liked.

☙ Don't be afraid to admit you don't know.

The three most important words in business are "*I don't know.*" I learned that early in my career when I was making a presentation to a client's new vice-president. I came in with the advertising, opened the boards, showed the layouts and read the copy.

Later the vice-president called; he came right to the point. "Why didn't you begin your presentation this morning with a statement of objectives?"

I said nothing.

"You do know what a statement of objectives is, don't you?" he snapped.

I paused, and then I said, "I don't know."

That vice-president went on to arrange a mini-business course for me and another person in his company, a course that laid the foundation for my first basic understanding of marketing principles.

"*I don't know*" literally changed my business life.

● Give your office your touch.

Maybe for you it's flowers on your desk or city photographs on your wall. Whatever, make it distinctive but not showy, pleasurable but not self-indulgent. (Please, no diplomas or awards.)

If you can assure yourself that it's something that will make other people feel good, you know it's the right touch.

● Challenge yourself.

If your job doesn't give you enough opportunity to experiment with your own talents and thinking, make your own demands on yourself. Learn French, take a word-processing course, try painting or Chinese cooking, or both. Do things that increase your skills, force you to use your brain. The more you use your brain, the better it gets. When you practice thinking just the way you practice tennis or skiing, you'll get a lot better.

▣ Don't gloat.

Nobody's heart goes out to someone who won, or got what everybody else wanted but didn't get.

▣ Don't make snap judgments about people or situations.

All first impressions are not perfect insights into a person's character and qualities.

Think carefully before you assign—or take away—responsibilities based on a first impression.

▣ Don't plant bombs under the idea that was used instead of yours.

And don't pout, stamp your foot, or complain in the ladies' room.

Smile, kid, smile, because that's the only way they'll let you back in to sell another day.

◀ Don't get stuck in a dead-end job.

If you think you are able to do your supervisor's job—
and do it better—and your supervisor stands like a road-
block to advancement, then now is the time to jump one
step and go to your supervisor's supervisor. Skip one on
the organization chart. Explain your qualifications and
state the reasons you can handle more work, and so save
money for the company. Don't be emotional, and don't
be petty. Above all, don't criticize the person you are
working for.

When you do this, you are, of course, laying your
job on the line. You're taking a calculated risk, rolling
the corporate dice. And somebody up there may not like
you for what you are doing.

But remember that it is often easier to advance in
the company where you already work than it is to start
at a higher level at a new place.

Sometimes you have to take drastic action to get
your career off dead center.

☙ Beware of the easy stuff.

Work tends to become mechanical after a while.

Because you may do one part of a job very well, you tend to do it quickly, brush it aside—after all, no one will look too closely.

But just think what new ideas you can hatch if you take the same kind of time on old jobs that you do on new.

You think the tough stuff will kill you. But easy things can do you in a lot faster.

☙ Find the niche that's right for you, and move into it as fast as you can.

Stockbroker Julia Walsh picked her niche soon after she entered the financial world; she wanted to be involved in the venture capital area of corporate finance. "But that just wasn't an area where women could operate years ago. I had the retail kinds of investors, women who thought they were making a big move if they bought American Telephone common instead of American Telephone bonds.

"Although I worked for a fine company that would have been receptive to the things I wanted to do, I knew I'd move a lot faster out on my own. Besides, my sons were interested in the business."

So, at the age of 53, in 1977 she formed Julia Walsh & Sons.

Today she travels the world, is a frequent guest on "Wall Street Week," and has seen her company grow to annual revenues of $3.5 million, with 35 employees, 4,000 accounts, and seats on the New York and American stock exchanges.

As for Julia Walsh herself, she's never been happier. She's in the middle of the high-tech and computer world and making her company grow.

⬤ Don't make career changes when you're emotionally upset.

The decision to stay or go should never be made when you are not in command of your emotions.

Before you take any action, decide coolly and rationally what that action should be. You should *not* leave a job if three of the following are true:

- you have been made aware of future growth plans and have been assured that they include you;
- you are learning in your job;
- your job is in the field for which you are qualified;
- the company has a reputation for treating employees fairly;
- the things that bother you are the same things that bother most of the other employees;
- your salary structure and benefits are fair;
- there is both challenge and reward.

▣ Entrepreneurialism begins at home.

American business is full of stories about women who began businesses in their own kitchens. The most famous is probably Margaret Rudkin, who founded Pepperidge Farm, the company she later sold to Campbell's.

Another among today's entrepreneurs who found a career at home is Betty Talmadge of Atlanta, once the wife of the governor of Georgia and later a senator's wife. After her divorce, Betty devoted her time to the meat-brokerage business she began with her husband. And now she has a second career—her home. The house where she lives in Atlanta was the inspiration for Twelve Oaks in *Gone With the Wind*, and Betty rents her house for special Atlanta events and has a waiting list of convention and local groups. Her next plan is to take over the house that inspired Tara, put in the movie front as the entrance to the house—and double her business.

▣ Decide whether your next step is as a six-figure business owner or a six-figure manager.

You've had some time to know yourself well. Do you do better working as a manager in a large organization, or do you prefer the freedom of operating alone?

Before making your next job change, ask if it should be a career change. Consider your own emotional satisfactions. Big business or your own venture? And which is right now? Think about your talents in these terms:

The large organization pleases me because
- I am most comfortable when dealing with structured business settings;
- I like being part of the team in the office;
- I appreciate the facilities and fringe benefits in a large company.

The ownership life is for me because
- I love the Sweaty Palm Syndrome of never knowing if I'll win or lose everything;
- I enjoy presenting my own ideas and living and dying for them;
- I want my independence, and I'm willing to be small and have fewer comforts and less assistance.

⬤ Don't burn your bridges.

It's a great temptation to tell the last boss in your life exactly what he or she does wrong. But what have you gained? A Los Angeles corporation consultant who worked for three major companies remembers, "Each time I left I was determined to leave behind a group of executives who were as aware of my contribution as I was of theirs. Because no matter how good any of us are convinced we are, somebody made that company grow before we got there. I've kept all my ties to old jobs, and there isn't a day that goes by that I don't use one of my old bosses as a reference; in fact, two of them have sent me business."

● **Keep an eye on the people above, below, and alongside you.**

Almost all promotions are made after an evaluation of your ability to work with others. This will always be true.

Elizabeth Hanford Dole, Secretary of Transportation, says in describing her chief asset that it is "the ability to understand, manage, and work with people on all levels of an organization."

She is quick to acknowledge those who have helped her most in her career—her parents; Dr. Earl C. Borgeson, who gave her her first job in Cambridge; and Virginia Knauer, who introduced her to her husband, Senator Bob Dole from Kansas.

Secretary Dole, in her present position, is responsible for program development, budget, and administration of a cabinet department with approximately one hundred thousand employees and a 25-billion-dollar budget.

● **Never announce your own promotion, raise, job change, assignment, or trip until it is signed, sealed, and delivered.**

Because, as we always say in our office, "Nothing is sold until it's sold."

III

THE
SIX-FIGURE
WOMAN

They arrive by different routes, these women of accomplishment. Some come up the corporate ladder, others are in the professions, and many are entrepreneurs. But each has this in common: no woman feels she did it alone. She has had mentors or supervisors or people who believed in her, and frequently they were men who were steps ahead of her on the corporate ladder.

The six-figure woman believes herself to be goal-oriented and considers being a woman her greatest asset as well as her greatest obstacle to success.

She tries to maintain her femininity in business but not at the risk of losing or compromising a business position. A tough-minded executive at work, she takes a limited number of vacations (averaging only thirteen days per year) because, like almost all of these achievers, she describes work as "fun." The six-figure woman has a divorce rate above that of the national average; she has children; she is over 40 and has encouraged her daughter(s) to be career-oriented with a goal of financial independence.

Books have influenced her development (everything from Colette, Zen literature, and Proust to Ayn Rand and Eric Hoffer). Interestingly, for as many women as have been shaped by their reading, an equal number can recall no book that has made a significant difference in their thinking or their lives.

She has many friends who are not as career-oriented as she and enjoys being with them, for she can relax, or as one woman said, "... kick off my shoes, put my feet up, have a little wine, and just dish without anyone grading my performance."

More and more, however, she turns to the increasing number of high-powered networking groups that permit executive women to meet on a regular basis both regionally and nationally.

The six-figure women of means are very different from women whose incomes are dependent on men of means.

In the late 1960s I wrote a book titled *Mrs. Success.* In it I described the lives and attitudes of women who were married to successful men. My conclusion was that while Mrs. Success had material things, she was often frustrated by her inability to use her superior education beyond an occasional volunteer committee, and she felt unappreciated because she believed that her social contributions were not nearly so important as her husband's material ones. While she knew she lacked recognition, Mrs. Success didn't think she deserved any.

The six-figure woman, of course, is very different in her life style and attitudes, yet she is not without complaints and concerns. She feels frustration, but for an entirely different reason. She is frustrated because the work at the office is never done, nor does responsibility end at the office. She is constantly concerned about her children, regardless of their age and place in life.

In a 1983 survey of female MBA's from Harvard ten years after graduation, *Fortune* magazine said, "Seasoned mothers... have learned some management lessons Harvard never taught." Chief among those lessons was the need for household help in managing both a career and home.

The six-figure woman also worries about her duties as a daughter and fulfilling her parents' expectations. She wonders if she is spending enough "meaningful time" with her husband and occasionally sneaks a peek at the women's magazines to see if there's some further clue to success at home.

Still, I did not interview anyone who would trade places with a stay-at-home woman.

In the office, the bottom line is what it's all about, and she knows it. This is still a time of trial and challenge. How can she continue to make a difference to the company? How can she help the company make or save money? What can she do that no one has ever done before? How can she bring her style into the management mix?

Since style is so much a part of the corporate world, let us consider the woman's style.

Florence Skelly has determined that there is such a thing as a female style in an organization, although it may not always be headed by a woman.

She describes a female-style company as one concerned with the here and now. She asserts that the female-style company is one that is devoted to making things happen each day (as opposed to concentrating on being the biggest or the greatest in the industry), doesn't take itself too seriously, and is deeply concerned with making life pleasant for employees.

The female-style corporate characteristics apply generally to white-collar industries (service companies, information organizations) and the places where one usually finds women.

Production industries (iron and steel, automotive, heavy manufacturing) are the basic male-style companies and are characterized by management that is concerned with where the business is going rather than how it is getting there.

Concludes Ms. Skelly, "Male companies are made up of the long-term dreamers, The Big Picture People. But no company can support the big dream unless it also has the short-term person who can get things done."

Why is it that we women qualify as the persons who can get things done?

Because we have a tendency to believe that nothing is too much to ask of us and because deep down we women really cannot tolerate disorder.

But, of course, there are other reasons we are tapped for success. We bring other qualifications to the corner office. It is these five-star qualities that make us six-figure women:

- **Extra intelligence**
  Not just the brightness that moved us up the ladder, but unusual intelligence that includes awareness of the outside world, total knowledge of one's own industry, a quickness and brightness that make it easy for us to understand both new and old procedures.

- **Leadership potential**
  An ability to solve problems, deal effectively with people, and act authoritatively.

- **Independent action**
  That talent and confidence that permits acting on one's own; the stuff that stars are made of.

- **Timing and talent**
  One must have both. The same talents at another time in the company's history might go both unnoticed and unrewarded.

- **Growth potential**
  We are the ones who ask a lot of questions and aren't above taking a course or a seminar, going to a class that will expand our views, increase our knowledge, and improve our special talents.

- **Recognition of company goals and willingness to share responsibility for reaching them**
  One of the biggest problems for many women is their anxiety when entrusted with the future, their uneasiness when moved from the fixing and fussing of everyday corporate life. But a six-figure woman

knows all eyes are on her. The calculators are flash-
ing figures, and she will continue in her role and
advance only so long as she earns more money for
the corporation than she takes from it.

But while money and bottom-line responsibility are
what put her in her new job, her rewards are beyond her
salary:

There is satisfaction in entering an exclusive club.
Only eight-tenths of one percent of full-time working women in the United States earn more than $25,000
(compared with 12 percent of men), so that gives you
some idea of how few women earn more than $100,000.
Since few women are six-figure women, those who are
get more than grudging respect from men. And even
though some men and women may be slightly envious
("Is she really that good?"), they pay attention to the six-
figure woman.

**The executive woman is the new heroine of our
society.**
Respect is given and attention paid to the woman
who works. She is the heroine of our recent magazines.
Our new best sellers and films are now showing working
women in a sympathetic light.
But it's not all private jets and designer clothes.
There is a dark side to success, too. The fear of success
now translates to a concern about whether it is right for
a woman to have this much power and authority in what
we still perceive as a male-dominated world.
For some, overcoming that fear is a trade-off.
Chemist Juliette M. Morgan, now in her sixties and vice-
chairman of GAF Corporation, a major conglomerate,
has said her advancement was slow, and she realized she
would have to stay single if she wanted to keep herself

in line for executive promotion. She says, "I knew I couldn't have it all."

There are marriages that sink under the weight of the two careers. Much as we talk about equality and shared responsibility between the sexes, there are a lot of old stereotypes that need revising before any real equality comes to the six-figure woman.

Because she is not on a par with men and is different from other women, she will be late to come to terms with the men in her life. Or, more important, the man in her life.

The six-figure woman has less time to call her own because more people have call on her time. She can't say no to the quick business trip to London. She has to work late to get the figures ready for the annual report. Her long-planned vacations must be delayed. Her job plays havoc with her home life.

And, if she has children, there is always the specter of the child who thinks Mom is too busy to care.

Do we hurt our children because we work? Probably. But we hurt them when we stay home, too.

Because the six-figure woman can afford child care and because she is more mobile than any other group of working women, she probably has to work harder to explain her life role and convince her children that she isn't escaping her responsibility by working, but is deeply concerned about their mother/child relationship.

It's seductive, this six-figure life.

And, if you can handle the personal side, life can be challenging, rewarding, and most fulfilling. Almost daily there will be new challenges, new problems, new opportunities—and new lessons to be learned.

◎ Negotiate your contract.

Most large companies insist on a contract. When a six-figure woman in a large conglomerate was asked to sign her new contract after a substantial raise, she said, "I don't want a contract." The corporate lawyers and officers became nervous. "But you must have one," they said. She kept refusing to sign until finally management gave her one with more benefits than she would have requested.

That's not a typical story, however. In negotiating a contract, make sure

1. You have a lawyer or negotiator representing you. No one can negotiate successfully for herself.
2. You are protected in case of the sale of the company (this is called The Golden Parachute).
3. You cover such unexpected events as illness, maternity leave, severance, personal time, expenses for life style (entertaining, transportation, travel).

◎ Make sure your division group has goals.

It doesn't have any? Then get them written immediately. It's amazing how many companies assume everyone knows the goals, but it's a continually surprising fact that many of the largest companies operate without corporate goals.

€ Make sure you're getting what you deserve and are not just settling for title or salary alone.

Perks (perquisites), the fringe benefits of the executive life, can be included as part of your compensation package. But the time to ask is before you accept the job or sign the contract. It's almost impossible to get perks added at a later date.

- What are some of the perks to consider?

- Pensions, annuities, medical plans, deferred compensation, stock options
- Accounting and legal services
- Company car
- Use of company plane
- Use of corporate apartment
- Club memberships
- Educational loans for children
- Home security system

◈ Write first-rate job descriptions.

Negotiate your job with the person to whom you report by means of a job description.

Then repeat the process with those who report to you.

A working job description is not a piece of paper to be filed and studied only when a job must be filled, but something one can consult every day. It provides a method of self-evaluation as well as a tool for staff review.

A good job description clarifies the following points.

Position: the title itself

Objectives: goals to be met by the person in that position (e.g., a chief financial officer might have as a primary goal "to provide accurate financial data to be used for tracking in decision-making in the short- and long-term goals of the corporation.")

Scope: those divisions of the company where the person will operate, the general area of responsibility

Status: explanation of the direct reporting relationship

Responsibilities: both general and specific

⬤ Review your staff on a regular basis.

Use the job description as a measure of performance.
And don't put aside reviews, particularly in a business
that you may own. Job reviews are important, no matter
the size of the staff.

Many of us women are inventing leadership; some
of us entrepreneurs never worked for Procter & Gamble
or General Motors, but we can take a page from their
manual.

A regular review of all employees is important for
two reasons:

1. It makes the employee better at the job;
2. It makes the employer better at her job.

⬤   Prepare budgets accurately and promptly.

Ask for all the help you need in putting together a sound,
workable budget. Assume you can't go back for more
money if you get into trouble, and budget for the unexpected.

Your real employer is the bottom line; no matter
how much the company loves your style and the spirit
you bring, the real mark of the executive is the ability to
plan for and produce profits.

≜ Fill the talent gaps at once.

You're good enough to get here, but are you good enough to stay?

Only if you plug the gaps. You must assess your strengths and weaknesses, and be honest with yourself. So take a deep breath and a clean sheet of paper. Fill it out in this way:

TALENT	STRENGTH	WEAKNESS
Finance		
Administration		
Production		
Marketing		

Now for the hard part.

You must analyze yourself carefully. How well do you function in these or other vital areas you name? How do you assess yourself? For example, in the financial area you may be very good at long-range planning and weaker in day-to-day administration of costs.

The solution? Find yourself a good accountant or treasurer or comptroller.

There's a grace period when you take a new job. The grace period ends the day your administration fails the person who hired you.

⬗ Do your forecasting the company way.

Every company has its own ideas about the words "short-range planning" and "long-range planning."

Make sure you know the timing for both. All forecasts should include:

1. Projected changes in the industry;
2. Projected changes in the company (new products or services, elimination of divisions, automation);
3. Increased manpower needs;
4. Increased space needs;
5. Increased equipment needs (everything from real estate to duplicating machines);
6. Decreased manpower, space, and equipment;
7. Changes in the employee benefit package.

≋ Make certain that employees are given objectives along with the job to be done.

One of the major reasons that jobs are done improperly (and so must be redone at subsequent waste of time and money) is that directions are often given improperly.

Too often people are told *how* to do the job.

The correct way to give an assignment is to:

1. State the objectives (tell what you want accomplished);
2. State the criteria (explain the standards for judgment);
3. State the rules (time and money).

When you take the *how* out of management, you give employees the right to independent and original thought, and that is the magic of management.

● Plan your office; don't just decorate it.

Before moving into or redoing an office, give a designer and/or architect a guide to your style, an outline with the following information:

1. Work area needs
    A. Amount of desk area (top work surface, drawers)
    B. Equipment (typewriter, phones, etc.)
    C. Storage (files, books)
2. Conference area needs
    A. Amount of seating
    B. Display areas
        1. Tables
        2. Walls.
    C. Kitchen equipment
3. Personal needs
    A. Private bath
    B. Makeup facility
4. Preferences
    A. Favorite colors
    B. Art
    C. Plants, flowers
    D. Use of personal objects (including photographs)

☙ Now that you have authority, act authoritative.

If you assume the traits of leadership, people will accept you in your new role. These are some of the traits:

1. You make decisions and announce them exactly when you promise you will;
2. You bring in new ideas or add people who generate excitement;
3. You find new ways to make money for the company;
4. You know your budgets line for line and insist they be the parameters for management of the business;
5. You support your people within and outside the company.

If you are hired to shake up the system, do it.

No one will believe you're the boss until you do one or more of the following:

1. Add a new division;
2. Lop off a present department;
3. Add new people or reassign and reward present employees;
4. Get rid of deadwood;
5. Change the method of accounting;
6. Change lawyers, accountants, or other outside services;
7. Ask a lot of questions, and demand answers by a certain date;
8. Get in touch with key people in your industry or city and arrange personal meetings;
9. Improve working conditions;
10. Update present benefit plans.

Don't overdo the humble bit.

Since you are at the top, you can assume you've earned it.

Unfortunately we have so few female role-models in positions of authority that often we act as if we are apologizing for our titles.

No apologies necessary.

⬥ Make good and efficient use of your secretary.

It is not wasteful, sinful or mean to ask a secretary to exchange panty hose, pick up the birthday present for your mother or call the caterer for available dates for your dinner party. If you think so, just stop and ask yourself what your secretary earns an hour and what you are worth to the company each working hour. Anything that makes your life run more smoothly is going to be dollars to the corporation. The more stress you avoid, the more solid work you do.

The primary function of the secretary to a six-figure woman is to take over all possible jobs, organize all aspects of the boss's life, and do it with a cheerful, helpful attitude that contributes to a pleasant, healthy, working atmosphere.

Your secretary should be instructed to:

1. Open and sort your mail;
2. Know names of all your frequent callers (as well as the names of their secretaries) and to respect the dignity of all callers (no first names);
3. Keep a telephone sheet (with duplicate) of all calls received, and make notes of follow-up action if necessary;
4. Greet your visitors (take their wraps, seat them, offer beverages if that's your office style);
5. Keep a visitors' list with daily reminders on your next action;
6. Maintain your calendar on a daily basis. It takes three calendars to run a six-figure woman: one on her desk, one for her handbag or briefcase, and one on the secretary's desk. All must be coordinated every working morning.
7. Keep your expense account up to date and accurate with your help;
8. Handle your personal checking needs, restaurant reservations, travel plans.

▤ In a partnership, realize that you can't be an equal equal.

Nothing confuses employees more than misunderstandings over the identity of the ultimate authority.

Reporting on a daily basis to two (or more) equal equals is not satisfactory. In fact, it's downright destructive. Partnerships can work best when one person has the ultimate (CEO) responsibility. That doesn't mean the other partner can't voice an opinion, but it does mean that everyone knows who has the last word.

To be the non-CEO equal partner takes patience, and the only way you can make it work happily is to have your duties as partner clearly defined and find some areas of the business where you do have the last word.

▤ Never be satisfied.

Deborah Szekely, the dynamic president/owner/founder of Golden Door, Inc. and Rancho La Puerta, the fitness resorts, believes that her chief asset to her company is her "curiosity and the questioning of why things are done as they are."

Mrs. Szekely's constant asking, "Is there a better way?" and her healthy dissatisfaction with the status quo keep her resorts growing and changing, the latest addition being a floating Golden Door aboard the QE2.

Szekely, more than any other one person, is responsible for the growth of the old-fashioned beauty spa into a health-related industry. A believer in exercise, relaxation, and good diet, Szekely vociferously advocates improvement of the quality of life.

☙ No risk, no reward.

There isn't a six-figure woman who doesn't know the real meaning of those words.

For many, like Betty Smulian, it has meant the risk of starting a business... and the reward of seeing it flourish.

A designer for manufacturers of dredges in Baltimore, and prior to that a designer and store-planner in Philadelphia, she started her company—Trimble House, designers and manufacturers of lighting fixtures—when a bank president told her fifteen years ago that he would lend her money for her business.

She took the risk, and today she runs her own multimillion-dollar company.

€ **Sniff the territory, and understand when you can't win. For instance, you can't win if:**

1. The chairman, the president, or the next-in-command doesn't really like your idea;
2. The chairman's wife had the same idea last week and was turned down;
3. Everybody in the company thinks they did it last year—and they all know why it didn't work then either;
4. They really can't afford it;
5. Somebody somewhere is using your idea as a way of testing his or her power in the office;
6. You don't address corporate fears.

€ **Now that you're setting salaries, don't reward your staff too often, too much, or too fast.**

As you remember from all your other jobs, the salary is a psychological tool. When people are moved up too fast and rewarded too handsomely, they become overconfident and create people problems throughout your company.

It's always better to keep early raises on the low side; you have room to be generous at a later date. Once you've raised people to the top of their salary level, you can't reduce the salary if you're not satisfied with their performance. You can only fire them.

✎ Try to find out how determined your staff really is.

One six-figure woman who supervises a sales staff plays a little game called *Ichi ni san chi goh*. It's named for the Japanese numbers one to five: ichi (1) ni (2) san (3) chi (4) and goh (5).

Four people stand in the four corners of a room; one stands in the middle. When the numbers are called—ichi ni san chi goh—everyone moves from his or her position to another corner; the person left in the middle is the loser.

"I learn a lot from that game," says the executive who plays it. "I can see who's faster, who is more analytical, more clever. I once played it and literally pushed someone out of a corner because I was so determined to have it. Watching how people play the game, I can tell who is determined enough to work Saturdays and Sundays, who would have the tenacity to start a business and take no salary.

"As I think about it," she mused, "I realize we haven't played it for a while at our office. I think it's time to do it again."

● Don't let rewards become automatic or they lose meaning.

Ellen Straus, the head of WMCA Radio in New York, has a special planning group culled from her staff. They work on new ideas for the radio station. One day Ellen noticed that one young woman in the group came late, had few ideas. The next meeting day she also arrived late and contributed nothing. After it happened a third time, Ellen Strauss told her she would have to drop her from the group.

Immediately after that two things happened: the young woman began writing memos filled with first-rate ideas for the station, and—when those ideas went into action and she was credited—everyone else in the special planning group sat up and began to work harder.

● Know all your major customers.

You should be on a first-name, telephone-calling basis with your counterpart at all companies who are your customers.

The best way to know those people—and ferret out their major concerns and delights with your organization—is to invite customers individually to that old standby, The Business Lunch. And don't rush to entertain only the new people; those who've worked longest with your company should be seen regularly.

☙ Follow your dream.

Sometimes it's a conscious dream, sometimes not. For Pansy Ellen Essman of Pansy Ellen Products in Atlanta, a dream she dreamed one night was the start of her business. Twenty years ago she dreamed that she was bathing her granddaughter on a sponge pillow. She woke up, created the pillow—and a $45-million business that today features a long product line including nursery lamps, baby food organizers, highchairs, strollers, hook-on baby seats.

"However," she adds, "I had worked in factories for years. If I had not, I wouldn't have been able to make my dream come true because all I ever heard was the reasons my idea wouldn't work. I knew *how* to make that pillow; no one else did."

☙ Don't let glib answers stop you.

There is a six-figure woman president whose company chairman, a male, says that had she been at the Bay of Pigs, the ill-fated venture never would have taken place. "She would have sat there," he says, "and she would have asked, 'How much did you say it cost?' 'Where are they going?' 'How many men did you say?'"

And the chairman added that the woman president would have asked all those questions while assuring everyone present that she totally agreed with the concept; she just had a few questions.

❦ The memo wars and how to win them.

Memo writing is so frequently a corporate badminton game that shuttlecock diplomacy now threatens costs, relationships, and actions.

Take the case of the Coca-Cola executives and the company float in the Rose Bowl Parade.

Executive No. 1 sent a memo to an associate which said, in effect, "I don't really know what the cost of our float is, but it should be about a million, and I think that's too expensive."

Executive No. 2 wrote back that while he was also uncertain of the price, he thought a Rose Bowl float was a good idea. And so the memos went—back and forth, forth and back—until, eight weeks and many memos later, all the correspondence was finally unearthed by Executive No. 3. He was the one who had been waiting for cost approval in order to build the float.

Frantic effort, outrageous overtime, and nervous phone calls finally resulted in Coca-Cola's participation. But it could have happened with one phone call eight weeks earlier. The real problem? It wasn't a proper subject for a memo. No memo should be used to tell what you do not know. The purpose of a memo is to speed the process of management, not to slow it.

Proper memo writing should include:

1. Report of action taken;
2. Next steps (this means "I will do it" or "I will assign it"). There should be no response to a memo unless one disagrees with the steps to be taken.

If one does not possess information (as in the Coca-Cola case), the memo should assign responsibility for getting the necessary facts.

Use your key executives to full advantage.

Don't place equals in competitive positions and expect team spirit.

Don't make threats unless you're willing to carry them out (if you tell someone he must hire an assistant by June or risk his own promotion, then have the guts to follow through come June).

And make sure that every one of your executives knows that you back him or her fully each time he speaks for the company. You can't relate well to your key clients and customers if you don't relate well to your executive staff.

Check your power regularly.

There's a very good business version of the medical stress test. It's the power test, the way to test and check your importance in the company at regular intervals.

To take the test, ask yourself these questions:

1. Do I have easy access to the CEO?
2. Is my input necessary for most of the company's key clients or customers?
3. Do people under me take care to check with me before proceeding, or do they ask my superior or associate?
4. Am I invited to luncheons, dinners, or other public events that show the world my position... or is someone else chosen to represent the company?

☙ Be friendly but not chummy with the people who work for you.

Employees are embarrassed when they know too much—and ultimately you are, too.

☙ Maintain tolerance toward men.

They are having difficulty dealing with us because, as Gloria Steinem says, "We have become the men we wanted to marry."

☙ Never answer gossip.

Because no matter what you say, people will believe whatever they feel like believing.

⬚ Don't brood over mistakes.

You have more people reporting to you now, more people who take their emotional cues from you.

So don't take mistakes to heart.

Sure, some things will go wrong. Smooth them out as best you can, and move to the next major event. Nothing good happens if you keep moaning about the past.

And don't blame yourself unduly. Harry Levinson, who runs the Levinson Institute in Cambridge, one of whose functions is the nursing of the psyches of chief executives, has said that getting angry with oneself is the core of stress.

⬚ Keep your eye on the game.

There are so many intriguing projects, so many interesting possibilities, that you may find yourself being lured from what you consider your primary business. Don't be diverted. The thing that made you a six-figure woman is the thing that will keep you a six-figure woman: determining priorities.

As Sally Gries, president of Gries Financial Services, Inc., a financial planning and investment company in Cleveland, says in describing one of the major assets of the executive, "It is the ability to focus and prioritize, and at the same time remain aware of the other considerations."

⬙ Don't play Suzy Stoic.

Yes, you can show your feelings. Yes, you can keep a doctor's appointment. Yes, you can postpone a meeting because you're tired, ill, cranky, upset, nervous, not in the mood.

Just because you do those things doesn't mean people will think you are weak and ineffective. As a matter of fact, they will think you're just human, and that may make you a lot more likable.

⬙ Find a personal philosophy to guide your life.

While success is a motivating force, it is not the only concern of the six-figure woman.

Almost every six-figure woman has been able to articulate her beliefs. Some mention God and reincarnation. Some talk about the need to help and interrelate with others inside and outside their families.

Said Jacqui Kendall, a radio-TV personality in Detroit, "Perhaps we succeed when we have the belief that one was given a gift (ability) from God and that one must realize the full potential of that gift. Without help from others, the going is tough, but without self-help it is impossible."

≡ Put yourself first.

"Certainly no one else will." Those are the words of Gwen M. Vallely, who sells stocks, bonds, and tax shelters for Smith Barney, Harris Upham & Co., Inc.

"I made a significant change in my life as a result of an insignificant event," says Vallely. "A party on New Year's Day, 1981, was canceled, and I decided to review personal expenses versus my earnings. I was shocked when I realized how little I was able to save. That's when I realized I had to do something else."

So this ex-credit analyst, director of tourism for New York City, and TV news producer shifted to her present career.

Two bits of advice she would give other women:

- No one hands you anything—you must *earn* it (or take it).
- You have no one to blame for your failures but yourself—and also no one to credit for your successes but yourself.

✇ Get to the point.

No long preambles. No Joan Rivers routines.

The only way to be succinct is to prethink your words. It takes a long time in business before you can do your best thinking in a meeting. So until you get to that time in your life when you can go into a meeting secure in your ability to think on your feet, it's better to consider your opinions in the privacy of your office—then air them when you can say precisely what you mean.

✇ Get a fresh perspective by changing your activity totally.

When fashion designer Carolina Herrara finds a sleeve or waistline problem too tricky to resolve, she does a 360° turn away from her desk.

"First I sing a little to myself to see if that will help. If that doesn't work," says the newest of the couture designers, "then I go for a walk and stop to eat something simple and lovely like Japanese food.

"Then when I come back to my office, if I still can't find my answer, I get down on my hands and knees and scrub. I am a very good cleaner; I always use ammonia.

"Maybe the reason I like to clean is that I have never had to. There are fourteen servants at our hacienda in South America, and we are rarely at home in New York, but still I find that physical activity and purposefulness a steadying force in my life, and during some of my most intense scrubbing come some of my best ideas."

☙ Stop insisting that everything can run without you.

It can't.

You are indispensable. Nobody else does things quite the way you do, and so long as the world knows you hold that job, no one else will be able to fill it.

There may come a time when someone else will have to take over, but everybody knows it won't be the same.

Every manager is unique, and she contributes more than knowledge and dedication. She also invests a portion of herself, and it is that investment that makes her irreplaceable.

☙ Be tough enough to leave any deal on the table.

T. S. Eliot wrote, "Between melting and freezing, the soul's sap quivers." Quiver all you want while negotiating, but never give up more than you should. You are really strong when the person with whom you're dealing is aware that you have a reputation for fairness—but also knows that you are not afraid to walk away from any deal.

⬗ Take five minutes each day to stop by the office of one of your staff.

You may have nothing more to say than a pleasant "Good day," but it reinforces a staff's own sense of worth to know that you're not an immovable object in that corner office and are willing to venture forth to see what the real people are all about.

⬗ Pick your battles.

Don't turn every disagreement into World War III. Save the heavy artillery for the battles over special projects, title, authority, and salary. Before you drop any bombs, be sure you've asked and answered these two questions to your satisfaction:

1. What's the best thing that can happen if I win?
2. What's the worst thing that can happen if I lose?

And if the worst is that you may be fired, rethink your position. Remember that you won't lose face if you back away or tread softly. Remember that if you're outside the corporation you won't get another chance. Sometimes it's better to lose this one so you can stay to fight another day.

● Don't expect rewards, praise, or thanks.

Not constantly, anyway. Vladimir Horowitz, the pianist, when asked if he still gets a kick out of applause at the end of a concert, answered, "It's the silence that matters, not the applause."

But if you don't get rewards, not ever, then look for another job where you will. Money is wonderful, but so is *psychic satisfaction*. And that's one of the biggest rewards of life at the top.

● Ignore your enemies.

Of course you have enemies—that's one of the curses of ambition and desire for excellence—but never give an enemy the satisfaction of recognition.

Nothing makes enemies shrivel and die faster than neglect.

Above all, don't look for revenge. Time takes care of pride, power, passion—and enemies.

● Follow your heart.

"I'm not your typical Stanford Business School graduate," says Debbie Fields, the owner and creator of Mrs. Fields' Cookies.

"I run my business on emotion. I care more about making people happy than I do about making money." But, in pursuing happiness, she has also managed to find a certain amount of fame and fortune.

Her thick, rich, chewy cookies are large-size because Fields believes that people might feel guilty eating twelve cookies, but won't if they eat just one. To start her business she researched the ways of the corporate world and made the best cookies she could. Still, no one bought any when she opened her first store in Palo Alto in 1977.

"So I just took my cookies and gave them away at Stanford. People were so surprised they followed me back to the store, and because they liked what I gave away, they bought."

Fields, the youngest of five daughters, has worked since she was thirteen. Her father, a welder, and her mother instilled the work ethic in their daughters. "I've been everything from a third-base ball girl for the Oakland A's to a worker in the boys' department of Mervyn's," she recalls. "And the only reason I was successful was because my parents taught me that if you really want something, you should go after it. And I decided that I'd go after everything I wanted as long as it made people happy.

"And what could be happier than cookies?"

◉ Always fight for the work, never for the people.

Fighting for the work is the best way to support the people.

◉ Now that you have the authority, don't create sexual ghettos.

Most of us women complain loudly when men put us into neat, little compartments. Now, whenever we can, let's get rid of the stereotypical thinking.

The most often-seen sexual ghetto is in the sales area where the male sales manager says to the female salesperson, "You take the Revlon account, and I'll take Merrill Lynch."

Playing the unexpected not only keeps employees on their toes, but it's often good for business.

So go ahead—hire a male secretary and a female sales manager.

⏚ Never think that you have to do what the rest of your industry is doing.

Ann Bassett, the president of Bassett's Ice Cream Company in Philadelphia and the fifth generation to run the family business, says, "Many people wonder why I haven't gone into store franchising. I know my strength is in manufacturing a quality product. It's what I do best. Now I am concentrating on getting my product distributed nationally. When that is accomplished, then I'll consider other ventures. But, for me, one step at a time."

⏚ Learn to fire yourself.

Once you've taken command, hire someone you can train—a person who can do the job as well or better than you.

That's how Evangeline Gouletas-Carey, a principal in numerous corporations and real estate ventures, runs her business life. "When I started in business with my brothers Nick and Victor, we each did it all. We had a small company," she recalled. "Nick was in charge of acquisitions and marketing; Victor handled financing and legal matters; and I was doing accounting and serving as controller. That meant that I had many jobs: administration, property management, interior decorating, public relations, refurbishing, and construction. I knew the only way I would have time for truly creative management would be to get rid of my jobs one by one. So I looked carefully and kept finding people who could do each job as well or better than I. Each time I hired someone and got rid of that job, we made more money."

Sometimes it's hard for women, who are used to doing all the housework, to understand that as soon as someone else does floors and windows the executive woman is free to dream, plan, and operate at her highest level.

⬙ Don't hire friends.

It changes the balance of your relationship.

⬙ Always hire the children of friends.

The children of friends are always terrified that the only reason you are hiring them is that you are friendly with their parents (somewhat true). So they work six times as hard as anyone else in the office to prove that they should have been hired on their own.

● Get rid of the dummies below you, and proceed cautiously with the ones above you.

No matter how high you climb in business, there's always somebody making decisions that affect your life. It can be a chairman or a client or a customer. But somewhere there's a dummy you have to fit into your career plan.

What do you do about the ones above you?

The first rule is to avoid them whenever possible, and deal with other equals who are more amenable to your thinking and style. While avoiding those less-than-talented people in the big offices, you wait for the corporate structure to change favorably for you.

But life being what it is, you can wait only so long. Therefore, if you see no change coming and no other way the company can make your life better, it's time to think about your next job.

● Don't take too much work home with you.

There is life after work. And sometimes you approach things fresher the next day.

♣ Don't give away the farm in order to keep an employee.

It has happened to everyone who runs a business. One day one of your most trusted and valuable employees—someone to whom you've been a mentor—tells you of a better job offer and gives notice.

At first you're stunned. How could this perfect person want any job but the one here? Then you get angry. What right does that rotten competitor have to go after your people? Then you get competitive.

And this is where I've made mistakes. I've given too much just in order to hold someone. I've given pay raises, an extra week of vacation, assorted perks, and gentle stroking. And, in the end, each time my corporate heart has been broken: those so appeased never live up to their new rewards.

Once people have used another company as a bargaining point, been re-wooed and agreed to stay with you, the balance changes. Now there's too much weight on the other end of the seesaw.

I find it more honest when an employee comes to me and says, "I've had another offer. I really don't want to take it. I'd rather stay here. This is what I need to stay with you." Under those circumstances, when I've opened the corporate pursestrings, I can't remember one time the person hasn't really been worth the investment.

≝ Don't delude the people who work for you.

Don't offer praise when it's not deserved because you think someone needs it. In the long run, you're hurting that person. I once employed a copywriter, a bright young woman who was never meant to be a copywriter, but because I thought she had intelligence, I kept encouraging her and telling her that her work was good.

The year I had to cut costs and reduce staff, I let her go. She couldn't understand the reason. And at that moment I couldn't begin to criticize her work.

She never did get a job as a writer again, and I never overpraised anyone again.

When it comes to reviews, you have the opportunity to be totally honest. And you owe it to the company and to the employee. Remember that it's sometimes better to fire someone than to give that person false hopes and an incorrect sense of security about his or her talents.

≝ When you have to fire people, do it yourself.

No firing is painless, but since it's often inevitable, do it as quickly as possible.

1. Always precede a firing by stating the objectives and qualifications for the job and explaining your reasons for finding the person unsatisfactory in meeting the job goals;

2. Give the terms of dismissal (date the employee is to leave, severance, accumulated vacation days);
3. If you are willing, offer references for future employment;
4. Permit the fired person to maintain dignity and pride (was any of the failure due to your miscasting him or her?);
5. Immediately inform co-workers about the date of departure.

You won't feel good when this is over; no one does, but if it's any help to your conscience, remember that oftentimes a firing permits a person to pursue a more rewarding career. And, so far as your company is concerned, someone who isn't performing at top level lowers the productivity and morale of others in your area.

⬤ Know how to cut losses.

Losing money?

Then cut what you can as fast as you can: adjust staff costs through firing, lowering salaries, or a combination of both; reduce or liquidate aged inventory; restructure prices; save on fixed costs through changing of hours (more daylight time means lower costs for electricity), subletting, elimination of divisions; reduce travel and expense budgets; defer capital expenses.

When you seek cuts, however, remember that you are also dealing with people, and their morale must be considered. Don't take out all the fringes that make business life with you more pleasurable, give your company a special spirit and the employees a zest that makes them more productive.

≣ Don't take no for an answer.

Bonne Bell, our first national client, hired us on our first call. Since that happened so early in our life, we thought that was what the agency business was like.

It wasn't.

It took nineteen years of telephone calls and door-knocking for us to become a Goodyear agency, three years of letters and calls to become a Clairol agency.

Why did it take so long? Because in each case they were trying to match our talents with their requirements. But we kept going back as we increased and improved staff and services—and then came the day when their needs matched our services, and lo and behold! we were hired.

The three best ways to get where you want to go are to persist, persist, persist.

≣ If you want to be a good manager, first be a good mother.

All the things a mother provides—comfort, praise, scoldings and motivation; entertainment, teaching, punishment and rewards—are what shape the basic behavior system for corporate interaction.

≋ Always check the safety hatch.

Before starting a new business or a new division, or launching a new product, make sure you have outlined all action steps with bail-out position at each level. If the business is new, the first loss is always the cheapest and the easiest.

Never continue operating a business or a division because you're "optimistic," and never never never use that seductive word to get your company to spend money.

The only business reason to spend money is to make money.

≋ Don't get defensive the first time someone calls you "tough."

Because you are.

You wouldn't be here if you weren't ambitious, aggressive, and tough.

The thing to remember, however, is that you can still be sweet, feminine, and friendly. Just remind the person who calls you "tough" that men don't always turn into monsters when they run companies, so why should women?

⬤ Don't let research make decisions.

Research is a tool of decision-making; it is not decision-making.

The world is full of ideas and products that tested badly, only to go to market and find a niche in the hearts and pocketbooks of the world.

Conversely, ideas that score well and break the bank in test situations often falter in the marketplace.

Research is a tool. Judgment is still the way businesses grow.

⬤ Just before you say something you may later regret, leave the room and write your side of the story.

Then wait twenty-four hours, and read what you've written. If you still feel the same way, go ahead and say it out loud or write it and send it.

If you have changed your mind, just think of the trouble you've saved.

≣ Reward yourself.

Remember back in the days when you made less than $25,000 you thought some things were luxuries (exercise classes, massages, vacations, new coats)?

Well, they're not. They're necessities.

We women are so caught up in the Puritan ethic that we have a hard time enjoying money.

So take time to have some fun with your money, and do what one six-figure woman does each time she buys something she used to call "frivolous." She pauses and asks herself, "If it all ends tomorrow, will people say I had a good time?"

≣ Don't listen to everything "the authorities" tell you.

Sometimes a lot of innocence beats a little experience.

Years ago, when our New York office was losing money, I was given six months to turn it around. Since I didn't know it couldn't be done, I did it with a group of very special people. Today we all agree that our accumulated wisdom would probably keep us from trying.

◀ Use your business to build your business.

One of the best ways to make money is to expand the business you already have. That's what Marsha Broderick, a successful Los Angeles interior designer, discovered.

Broderick often hired construction companies for kitchen and bath alterations and house additions for her interior design work. When those construction people frequently failed to get to the job site on time—or failed to show altogether—she decided to put together an all-female construction company.

Pink Ladies is an organization of tradeswomen. They are easily identified by their pink T-shirts decorated with the company logo: a rose and a hammer.

The women work construction jobs throughout California, and early in 1983—from a field of 750 candidates—Pink Ladies was awarded the biggest job in its history, the multimillion-dollar renovation and relocation of the presidential mansion at Pepperdine University.

◀ Don't turn down an idea until you know who fathered it.

Is that politics?

Probably. But whoever said survival isn't often political?

€ Approach problem-solving creatively by putting together the least likely combination of possibilities.

Will you come up with something unique? Not necessarily. The important thing is that you will have exercised your mind and challenged yourself to go beyond the usual.

I like to write a problem in longhand at the top of a yellow page. Then I write down all possible solutions. There's something about a list that makes you write more lists. There is something about seeing your thoughts in writing that seems to stamp them more firmly in your mind. Sometimes I can close my eyes and see the list. It stays printed in my mind. And so that list, seen or unseen, often leads me to the idea I need just when I least expect to get it—when I'm in the theater or walking down the street or in a plane.

But what one learns about creativity is that the truly creative thoughts come to you only in the areas of your own intense thinking. Ideas come because one has spent some serious time concentrating on what needs to be done.

✑ When you're a director of a company other than your own, remember that you're wanted for your fresh viewpoint.

If that also means the woman's perspective, what's so bad about that?

Aileen Mehle (better known as the columnist Suzy) is a director of Revlon. At a shareholders' meeting, one woman stood and addressed the chairman, Michel Bergerac. "Sir," she said, "you have only one woman on this board."

"Ah yes," said M. Bergerac, "but what a woman!"

Comments Ms. Mehle, "Those of us who are not bankers, lawyers, and big corporate thinkers have contributions to make, too. We're not rubber stamps; we're not carbon copies. We're women."

✑ Don't turn down any offers of help.

Even though you don't need or want help, the donor sees it as his or her good deed. So learn to say, "Yes, thank you," with grace.

Otherwise you trivialize both the person and the deed, and once you do that, everyone knows you can't run the railroad.

€ **Repeat nothing—absolutely nothing—that is told you in confidence.**

There is no such thing as telling just one person.

€ **If you can't add to the discussion, don't subtract by talking.**

€ **No surprises!**

Don't hold back the good sales news or, more particularly, the cancellations.

Let it roll. Or you may be the one who's surprised.

⬤ Fight for your title.

You think I didn't have to because I was an equal owner of the business?

Wrong.

I didn't become president until 1979 because for most of the preceding years I bought the story that titles don't matter. Finally Lois Gould, the author, said to me one day, "If titles don't matter, then why doesn't the president give you his?"

That was the logic I used—and it won me the title.

Thank you, Lois Gould. Sometimes it takes somebody who doesn't know anything about your company to give you the clearest insights.

⬤ Bite the bullet, and make plans to change jobs if:

1. You have irreconcilable differences with person(s) to whom you report;
2. You are being excluded from important meetings— a sure sign your days are numbered;
3. You are not consulted on major policy decisions;
4. You are not invited to represent the company at significant public events;
5. You have no room to grow (the person ahead of you is your age, or your particular kind of talent is undervalued in the company).

☙ Never compromise quality.

"The work ethic changes as you change," says Rose Narva, now president of Murdock Hotels. "I've learned that women, as they get more responsibility and occasionally earn more money, have to become more sensitive and more aware of the game plan. You have to be prepared, watch for the pitfalls, be on your toes, and justify all actions—because once we begin to move up, we women become very threatening to men.

"One thing we cannot give up, however, is our own vision, our quality perceptions. I've left two jobs because I wouldn't compromise quality. I managed a hotel and was told by the owners, 'Don't treat it like it's yours because it's not.' That night I went home and told my son and husband I was leaving the position."

Ultimately it was her reputation for running quality operations that caused David Murdock to name Narva president of his developing hotel chain. Within twelve months Narva supervised the design and building of the new Baltimore Harbor Court, part of an estimated $100 million hotel-condominium-office project, and worked on the Cornhusker, a rebuilt hotel in Lincoln, Nebraska. She spends one week a month in Los Angeles at corporate headquarters.

"Unfortunately there's a real stigma for the attractive woman in the executive suite," said Narva. "First is the assumption that one must be a p.r. person, and second is always the question—said with a special intonation— 'And how did you get here, little girl?'"

◀ Always keep some "walking-away" money in reserve.

The smart woman is the woman who isn't afraid to turn down any job unless it does for her what she thinks it should. That doesn't mean she always goes for the dollars. She doesn't have to. She always has a little walking-away money in reserve.

Just knowing the money is there lets you behave differently. I don't know why—maybe it's instinct—but people always sense when you're just a bit hard to get. And that makes them want you all the more.

◀ Use your talent for something besides your own business.

And give it away.

You increase your sense of self when you give something to the community that has made you grow and flower. It's the best kind of thank you.

AFTERWORD

There has never been a better time to be a woman, so go ahead and—

Make the most of every day.

There is a six-figure woman who wakes each morning and bounds out of bed convinced that something wonderful is going to happen. By five o'clock, if nothing wonderful has happened—she makes it happen.

And that is what sets the six-figure woman apart from all others: she is the one who makes things happen.